DEATH
set to Music

Masterworks by
BACH
BRAHMS
PENDERECKI
BERNSTEIN

Paul S. Minear

John Knox Press
ATLANTA

Acknowledgment is made for permission to reprint:

To The American Scholar: Reprinted from THE AMERICAN SCHOLAR, Volume 51, Number 2, Spring, 1982, Copyright © 1982 by Elder Olson and Volume 52, Number 2, Spring, 1983, Copyright © 1983 by Leon Kass. By permission of the publishers.

To Jacques Barzun for excerpts from *Pleasures of Music* (New York: Viking, 1951). By permission of Jacques Barzun.

To Mrs. William D. Donnelly for excerpt from a letter to her father, published in R. H. Winnick, ed., *Letters of Archibald MacLeish, 1907 to 1982* (Boston: Houghton Mifflin, 1983). By permission of Mrs. William D. Donnelly.

To Alfred A. Knopf, Inc. for excerpt from Wallace Stevens, "Sunday Morning," *The Collected Poems of Wallace Stevens*, copyright 1968. By permission of Alfred A. Knopf, Inc.

To the National Council of the Churches of Christ in the U.S.A.: Unless otherwise indicated, Scripture quotations are from the Revised Standard Version of the Holy Bible, copyright 1946, 1952, and © 1971, 1973 by the Division of Christian Education, National Council of the Churches of Christ in the U.S.A. and used by permission.

To The New York Times for excerpt from H. C. Schonberg, "Low-Key Celebration for a Master" (*The New York Times Magazine* [24 April 1983]). Copyright © 1983 by The New York Times Company. Reprinted by permission.

To Ovation for excerpt from Ray Robinson's November 1983 interview of Krzysztof Penderecki. By permission of publisher.

To Simon and Schuster for excerpt from Leonard Bernstein, *The Joy of Music*, copyright 1959. By permission of publisher.

To Time for excerpt from William Bender, "A Mass for Everyone, Maybe" (20 September 1971). Copyright 1971 Time Inc. All rights reserved. Reprinted by permission from TIME.

Library of Congress Cataloging-in-Publication Data

Minear, Paul Sevier, 1906–
  Death set to music.

  Bibliography: p.
    1. Music—Religious aspects—Christianity.   2. Death—
Songs and music—History and criticism.   3. Bach,
Johann Sebastian, 1685–1740.   Matthäuspassion.
4. Brahms, Johannes, 1833–1897.   Deutsches Requiem.
5. Penderecki, Krzysztof, 1933–   . Passio et mors
Domini nostri Jesu Christi secundum Lucam.
6. Bernstein, Leonard, 1918–   . Mass.   I. Title.
ML2900.M5   1987   783'.09   86-45352
ISBN 0-8042-1874-9

© copyright John Knox Press 1987
10 9 8 7 6 5 4 3 2 1
Printed in the United States of America
Atlanta, Georgia 30365

To
The Choir
of
The First Congregational Church
in
Guilford, Connecticut

ACKNOWLEDGMENTS

This manuscript was prepared during a residency at the Rockefeller Foundation Study Center in Bellagio, Italy. I am grateful to the Foundation and to the staff of the Villa Serbelloni for that productive and enjoyable period. In chapters two and three, Professor Jon D. Bailey has made many astute suggestions, based on his experience in directing those choral works, and I thank him for those suggestions. In this, as in all my writing, I have received enormous help from my wife.

Contents

DEATH set to Music

O may I join the choir invisible
Of those immortal dead who live again
In minds made better by their presence: live
In pulses stirred to generosity,
In deeds of daring rectitude, in scorn
For miserable aims that end with self,
In thoughts sublime that pierce the night like stars,
And with their mild persistence urge men's search
To vaster issues . . .
        This is the life to come,
Which martyred men have made more glorious
For us who strive to follow. May I reach
That purest heaven, be to other souls
The cup of strength in some great agony,
Enkindle generous ardour, feed pure love,
Beget the smiles that have no cruelty—
Be the sweet presence of a good diffused,
And in diffusion ever more intense.
So shall I join the choir invisible
Whose music is the gladness of the world.[1]

Prelude

Whether or not music is the oldest of the arts, it is surely the most fully universal as well as the most widely enjoyed. From the contented coo of the infant to the somber pulse of the funeral dirge, music forms a parenthesis in sound that encloses the story of each human being. It can transmute the entire range of emotions and yearnings, from the spontaneous explosion of inner excitement to the routine rendition of the national anthem.

> Music nowadays, whether we like it or not, is interwoven with the texture of our lives from morning till night. Music resounds for, with, and through everything; it is canned and broadcast, recorded and rebroadcast; it is, so to speak, piped into our houses at the very time when it has virtually ceased to be piped within them.[2]

Whether we think of music as the work of professionals or as the avocation of millions, we can probably agree that it has the strange capacity to turn "passion into sound" and "sound into passion." No agony is too stunning, no joy too ecstatic, to escape expression in some aria or alleluia. Sensitive composers can cast a magic spell around unnamed griefs in such a way as to release a nameless joy. They can do many things that spoken words can never do. Their harmonies can resolve discords in distraught spirits, as their rhythms can correct the arrhythmia of ailing hearts. Composers are translators of the basic texts of human experience.

> Music, oldest of arts,
> Unlike all others
> Moves immediately upon the mind,
> Presents no Lear for pity,
> No awakening Adam for wonder;
> We exult or grieve, unable to say why;
>
> Nor can we say how it was
> That suffering, thought, toil
> Became the fleeting touch of a fingertip,

> How the insensate instrument
> Shook the insensate air
> To make passion into sound, sound into passion.
>
> How a man became music,
> We became that music,
> All the many listeners became one,
> Differences like discords
> Resolved in concord.[3]

In setting the human story to music, composers do more than embellish that story with fancy embroidery. They tell the story, and in telling it, reveal insights that would otherwise remain undisclosed. And to the degree that mortality is integral to that story, setting death to music becomes integral to the vocation of composers. There is, accordingly, nothing strange about the fact that requiems and masses hold a central place in the history of Western music.

The Western musical tradition has, for centuries, appropriated and interpreted the biblical story, that saga that links archetypal details to mythological drama. That saga accords primary, even cosmic, significance to two deaths, those of the first and the second Adam. This being true, the Bible itself might be properly called the human requiem, a Christian "Book of the Dead." Its pages articulate every kind and degree of suffering, every perceptible intimation of mortality. Within that segment of the Bible that Christians revere as Scripture, the New Testament, readers may discern many unexpected and even paradoxical perceptions of death. For instance, these authors often speak of their own deaths in the past tense; they view themselves as "dead men on holiday." Virtually every page in the four Gospels anticipates Jesus' Passion as the intended climax of his work. The Epistles dwell long and variously on the implications and consequences of that Passion. They take for granted the requirement that every believer must share in the suffering of the Lord. As a summation of their deepest conviction, the aphorism is fully justified:

> The whole world is Calvary writ large . . .
> a man's soul is Calvary writ small.[4]

It is because the New Testament authors are so obsessed with the story of Jesus that their perceptions of mortality take on such protean shapes and disguises.

Because of their obsession, composers of all centuries who have sought to set biblical themes to music have been impelled to set death to music. The translation into music of human experiences of mortality has linked them to the comparable preoccupation of Christian apostles and prophets with the Passion of Jesus. On the one hand, their requiems cannot be fully appreciated apart from the vast reverberations of the biblical story of Calvary. On the other hand, that story can seldom be fully appreciated until it is set to music by master sensors of the human spirit. Composers are such superb interpreters of experiences of mortality, whether in modern life or in ancient literature, that all other interpreters of the same texts would do well to listen acutely to them.

Whether or not such generalizations are true for all composers, they are undeniably true for the four musicians whose works are the subject of study in the chapters that follow. These four have been gloriously obsessed with the texts, both the contemporary and the biblical. They use biblical librettos and therefore become subject to exegetical analysis; they use musical language and therefore become subject to compositional analysis. Accordingly, practitioners of both academic disciplines are needed. Unfortunately, however, there is a wide chasm between those disciplines, one that is steadily growing wider. Virtually no scholar can be cited who is equally adept in both. Very early in this century one could name Albert Schweitzer, whose epoch-marking books on the New Testament were matched by his two-volume study of J. S. Bach.[5] Even in Schweitzer's work, however, it would be difficult to speak of a genuine union of the two disciplines. His interpretations of Jesus and Paul show no strong evidence of his musical sensitivities, and his analysis of Bach's music profits only occasionally from his training as a biblical exegete. Even so, this exegete-musician has had no successors in his dual role. Certainly I make no such claim for myself. These pages are penned by an exegete and not, definitely not, by a musicologist. Consequently, in what follows, I speak primarily to other interpreters of Scripture, urging more sustained attention to composers who interpret biblical texts by way of music. Should musicians also find value in looking afresh at these composers in the light of their biblical exegesis, I shall, of course, be gratified.[6]

In what follows, the procedure is quite straightforward. In chapter one I seek to establish a base of operations by charting the range of attitudes toward death that characterize New Testament authors. In the next four chapters I examine four musical works to trace the influence of those biblical attitudes on the composer's interpretations of mortality. As you read those chapters, I urge you to have at hand recordings and librettos (preceding chapter text) of the selected works, so that you, too, may follow the movement of thought from biblical text to music, and back again.[7] If you can gain access to the orchestral and choral scores and use them as you listen to the music, your study will be all the more profitable.

The Baseline of Christian Thought

The roots of Christian thinking about death reach deep into the soil of the Bible. Yet when we turn to the Bible, we may well be baffled by the infinite number and variety of attitudes toward dying. We notice immediately that the metaphorical use of many nouns and verbs tends to drive out precise literal meanings; as a consequence, ideas about mortality proliferate helter-skelter. Concepts are vague rather than precise; meanings shift rather than remain fixed. Because of this apparent exuberance and confusion, I wish at the outset to distinguish and to classify some of the dominant variants.

Beginning with the biblical material is appropriate for two reasons: the composers themselves began by selecting biblical texts for setting to music, and the earliest musical treatments of the death of Jesus are to be found within the New Testament itself. If you find this chapter too technical or too peripheral to sustain your interest, you may wish to shift at once to the study of the composers. If so, I urge you to return to this chapter after finishing the others, for listening to the music should enhance your grasp of the intrinsic meanings of the biblical texts, and those texts should in turn enhance your appreciation of the music.

To begin, consider this basic distinction: some biblical perceptions of death coincide with perceptions common to nonbiblical thinkers; other biblical perceptions are alien to nonbiblical thought. I will examine first the shared perceptions and then those that are more alien and therefore less intelligible.

First is the most common perception of all: death as an event within the context of an individual person's story, marking the end of that story as birth marks its beginning. Although medical experts may differ in determining the exact moment when this event takes place—the heart stops beating, the lungs breathing, the brain functioning—virtually everyone uses the word *death* to refer to this event as a medical fact. There is also wide agreement about its universality and its inevitability, though, of course, no one can know with certainty what happens or does not happen to the person therein. This use of the term is common throughout the Bible. New Testament authors adopt without demur the realism of Isaiah: "All flesh is like grass and all its glory like the flower of grass" (1 Peter 1:24; cf. Isa. 40:6–9). They flatly repudiate any inclination to claim immunity to the fate of plants and animals. An Indian proverb would be quite at home in the Bible: "Death is the black camel that kneels before every door." The story of Jesus' death in the Gospels employs the term with this austere meaning: "We have a law, and by that law he ought to die" (John 19:7). Any suggestion that Jesus did not die in this sense of the word is repudiated. The same candor applies to thinking about believers; they had no more right than their master to claim immunity to death. It is true that some texts may be interpreted as supporting the expectation that we shall not all die (1 Cor. 15:51; John 11:25); but the same authors in other texts discourage us from making very much of that expectation (Rom. 7:2; John 11:25). As medically defined, then, death is everywhere in the Bible accepted as a destiny of "all flesh."

Here, however, I must underscore the fact that there is something quite unusual in the New Testament use of the term in this sense. Only in relatively few instances do the nouns and verbs for dying bear the medical definition as their primary denotation. A wide range of other denotations and connotations dominates early Christian thinking, as you will see. By contrast, nonbiblical attitudes toward death are dominated by the normal medical definition. Kübler-Ross' book *On Death and Dying* speaks of death in the standard way, only as a medical fact, understood if not welcomed by everyone. Death is treated as "the biggest crisis people had to face"; thus, the major relevance of religion consists of its assurance of life after this death.[1] The same concept dominates the selection of extracts in *The Oxford Book of Death*.[2] It is proper, of course, that an anthology of attitudes toward this theme should be based on the prevailing nonbiblical definition of the term; that, presumably, is why many significant New Testament sayings about death are ignored. When an anthology editor accepts the standard concept as the norm, it is quite in order that he or she should include chapters on suicide and on the death of animals, topics that are almost wholly absent from the New Testament. Such an editor also collates colorful quotations on such cognate topics as farewells, funerals, epitaphs, and cemeteries. The New Testament treatments of death rarely reflect such concerns. Why not? Surely because the normal conceptions of death, though not wholly absent, have moved from the center of concern toward the periphery.

A second way of thinking about death offers a point of contact between biblical and nonbiblical cultures. In this approach, the terms for death and dying are applied not to the terminal event itself but to a person's anticipation of that event, especially to the fear of it.

> Cowards die many times before their deaths;
> The valiant never taste of death but once.[3]

Shakespeare is right, as usual. Moreover, we should agree that the many deaths suffered by cowards fully deserve the word *death*. For them the image of the Grim Reaper is, in fact, more terrible than the event itself. Another poet suggests some of the effects of this fear:

> Death, and his image rising in the brain,
> Bear faint resemblance; never are alike;
> Fear shakes the pencil; fancy loves excess;
> Dark ignorance is lavish of her shades:
> And these the formidable picture draw.[4]

Biblical writers are as familiar with "the image rising in the brain" as are secular writers. Consider, for example, this thought-complex from the epistle to the Hebrews:

> Since therefore the children share in flesh and blood, Jesus likewise participated in the same nature, so that by dying he might destroy him who wields power over death (the devil) and deliver all those who through fear of death were subject to lifelong bondage. (Heb. 2:14–15, author's translation)

Because this writer perceives that the fear of death is a greater enemy than death itself, he also seeks deliverance from that fear as more desirable than deliverance from death. This is a perspective intelligible to people of every century and culture. It is true, of course, that this epistle speaks of slavery and deliverance in a distinctively biblical way: the devil uses death to instill fear; fear establishes a bondage to the devil; Jesus' death exerts power to break that bondage.[5] However, when this writer gave priority to the fear of death, he spoke for many others who would have little sympathy with these distinctive convictions.

A writer who has recognized such priority is Ernest Becker:

> Of all things that move man, one of the principal ones is his terror of death.[6]

That terror is universal and can be found operating within persons who are quite unconscious of it or who believe they have overcome it. It lies at the root of other fears and hides within all of them.[7] In an effort to gain immunity from terror, a person may resort to devious means of self-deception and repression: psychological tricks, aesthetic diversions, social games, obsession with one's career. Becker finds that the most effective insurance against the terror is gained through pursuit of moral excellence and religious devotion. Prevailing forms of religious observance can anesthetize the inner anxieties. So Becker traces evil, not to the event that terminates life, but to the many ingenious subterfuges by which we evade and deny death. Such denial becomes a form of death worse than the event itself.[8]

Having noted two basic points of convergence between biblical and nonbiblical definitions of death, I will now turn to some divergent definitions. These often become so subtle and so metaphorical as to elude verbal capture, and a student is tempted to challenge the legitimacy of using death-terminology at all. Yet the authors undoubtedly chose such terminology because they considered it essential for conveying their thought. A student must therefore make an effort to understand why they used *death* for events, acts, and emotions that are rarely treated as being so final or so disastrous.

A first example is offered by the close interdependence of two concepts, death and sin.[9] In the thought of St. Paul, death-in-sin and death-to-sin were phrases pointing to inescapable realities. Quite obviously these deaths are not the same as medically certified dying, yet Paul viewed them as even more significant. To grasp the reasons why he did so, one's own thinking must become more flexible. Paul clarified the meaning of one of these phrases by referring to Jesus: "The death he died he died to sin" (Rom. 6:10). Although he is not denying that Jesus died on Golgotha, Paul is speaking about another and more decisive death that took place before Golgotha, within the hidden recesses of Jesus' mind and will. Of course this death-to-sin led to Golgotha, but that is not the primary thing. The primary thing had to do with this person's relationship to God and to potential rebellion against God, i.e., sin. To Paul, what a person dies *to* defines who he is in an ultimate sense. "So you also must consider yourselves dead to sin and alive to God in Christ Jesus" (Rom. 6:11).

Death-in-sin is a phrase that conveys almost the opposite thrust. Consider Paul's ejaculation: "sin revived, and I died" (Rom. 7:9). Paul, alive, is speaking of Paul, dead. He speaks in total seriousness. In saying this, Paul does not separate death from sin in time or place, as something that is inflicted on a person as God's subsequent punishment for an earlier act. No, it is when a person sins that he or she dies. It may be debated whether Paul was speaking of choices made before or after his conversion, but the logic holds firm. Death and sin occur simultaneously, and both are within a person's own control. To cope with Paul's thought, readers must alter their perceptions of both sin and death. His thinking is not unlike that of the psalmist for whom a sinner's throat "is an open grave" (Rom. 3:13; cf. Ps. 5:9). To give due weight to that figure, a maximum flexibility in both language and imagination is required.

A third step logically follows: it is such death-in-sin that discloses the strategic necessity of death-to-sin. To those who have died in sin, the gospel offers the opportunity of dying to sin. This is precisely what belief in Jesus means: "we have been united with him in a death like his" (Rom. 6:5). "How can we who died to sin still live in it?" (Rom. 6:2). Because both death-in-sin and death-to-sin are viewed as taking place before the end of natural life, it would be easy to treat these biblical notions as wholly metaphorical and hence as much less significant than the literal notion. But to do that would make an understanding of biblical thought impossible. Not only did these authors consider these figures of speech important, they also preserved the nexus between the figures and the realm of actual happenings, both in the story of Jesus and in their own stories. Yet, to make these metaphors a baseline for our own thinking is quite another matter. Such use of language is so radically different from the conventional use that it must be either utter nonsense or an inspired revelation of the way in which God views things, the God who says, in this as in other matters, "For my thoughts are not your thoughts" (Isa. 55:8).[10]

The same is true of two other axiomatic convictions about death. Recall Paul's declaration: "The sting of death is sin" (1 Cor. 15:56). What is the meaning of the term *death* in this context? Here we may seem to be on familiar ground because the Apostle seems to be referring to the mortality and perishability of "the man of dust," our physical inheritance from the first human beings. But, again, the link to sin impels us to change the perspective. To accept Paul's declaration as true requires us to answer two questions. How do we usually measure death's sting? Our answer might be grief, aloneness, separation, injustice, cruelty, fear, oblivion. But normally we would not include sin in this list. And the second question: what happens to Paul's idea of death when it has lost its sting? Now death offers no threat, induces no terror. To Paul it is because of sin that death produces fear and establishes its dread power over the living. Here Paul uses Adam as a model that has been followed by all his descendants. Through Adam's death-in-sin, death's jurisdiction over all flesh was established (Rom. 5:12). A death-to-sin displaces that fatal legacy and draws the sting out of death. Is this nonsense or a truth that stretches the mind?

Paul adds another axiom to his analysis of death: "the power of sin is the law" (1 Cor. 15:56). By establishing this connection between the law and sin, the Apostle also linked the law to death. He was not speaking, of course, about laws in general but about the sacred covenant between God and Israel. How then did Paul conceive of the law's power to produce death through sin? One answer is given on an autobiographical and psychological level: "Yet, if it had not been for the law, I should not have known sin" (Rom. 7:17). God's prohibition of greed had become an incitement to greed. Thus a commandment that promised life had "proved to be death to me." So Paul's death-in-sin had become an instance of death-through-the-law. Accordingly, when Paul died to sin, he had also "died to the law through the body of Christ" (Rom. 7:4, 10–11).

To Paul this psychological level was also grounded in the historical experience of Israel. Looking backward, Paul viewed Moses' introduction of the law as an act separating two epochs. In the earlier epoch, death had reigned because of Adam's sin, although in the absence of the law, that sin had not been "counted." But the law had come in "to increase the trespass." It had given new inducements to sin and had made sinners more culpable; yet, all the while it had provided them with new opportunities to deceive themselves by encouraging hypocrisy and self-righteousness (Rom. 5:6–21). So the dispensation of the law had from the beginning been a historical epoch ruled by death, a death-through-the-law.

Paul was convinced that this fateful historical death-through-the-law had been overcome. He arrived at this conviction by pondering the story of Jesus' death as a revelation of God's own attitude toward the law. By the judgment of the law, Jesus had been a sinner, for the law declared that whoever "hangs on a tree" is accursed (Gal. 3:13; see also Deut. 21:22–23). So, in effect, God "made him to be sin" (2 Cor. 5:21). This Pauline view was consistent with that of the Gospels, in which Jesus is viewed as openly challenging the law and encouraging disciples to break it. The story of the crucifixion thus disclosed a double link between law and death: in dying the death commanded by the law (John 19:7), Jesus died to the law. Again we encounter invisible and mysterious forms of death, concealed in the depths of personal and social history. Ordinary perceptions fail to do justice to the forms that emerge when the story of Jesus is made the starting point for reflection and revelation.

Another way in which New Testament attitudes toward death clash with any common attitude is the habit, almost universal, of treating *death* and *life* as mutually exclusive terms. Where life is, there death has not yet arrived; where death strikes, there life ceases. Again, the story of Jesus produced a different pattern of thinking. Speaking for the living Lord, the prophet declares:

> "I died, and see, I am alive forever
> And I hold the keys of Death and Hades." (Rev. 1:18, author's
>   translation)

That declaration corresponds to predictions made by Jesus:

> "The Son of man will be delivered into the hands of men, and they will kill him; and when he is killed, after three days he will rise." (Mark 9:31)

In the Gospel of John this dying and this living are even more closely tied: the moment of Jesus' death is referred to as the moment of the most decisive change in human affairs.

> "Now is the judgment of this world, now shall the ruler of this world be cast out; and I, when I am lifted up from the earth, will draw all men to myself." (John 12:31–32)

When the same hour marks both humiliation and glorification and when the same event marks both defeat and victory, changes in vocabulary become imperative, at least among those whose vocation stems from that hour; that event and those changes will penetrate the range of metaphors that are adopted. So, for disciples of Jesus, life begins in the acceptance of dying:[11] "If anyone would come after me, let him deny himself and take up his cross . . ." (Mark 8:34). Thus Christ's declaration through the prophet, "I died, and see, I am alive" (Rev. 1:18, author's translation), is matched by the prophet's "dying, and see, we are alive" (2 Cor. 6:9, author's translation). Both statements define this form of dying as the point at which life begins.

When the term *death* is used to signal the emergence of life rather than its end, the term is often qualified by the preposition *for* or the phrase *for the sake of*. Jesus' death was essentially qualified by being a death "for God" and "for us"—for us, not as followers deserving reward, but as sinners in need of forgiveness, or even better, as murderers in need of amnesty. The same principle applied to his disciples, who were called to give themselves "for my sake and the Gospel's." Paul's suffering brought this vicarious principle home to him: "death is at work in us, but life is at work in you" (2 Cor. 4:12, author's translation). In suffering for others he carried in his body the dying of Jesus, "so that the life of Jesus may also be manifested in our bodies" (2 Cor. 4:10). No death that is not for others can manifest that life. In fact, a death for others is not the same as a death from which that for-ness is missing. Moreover, in the New Testament such dying for others is not simply a matter for individuals; it applies as fully to the church as to its several members. This communal dimension is basic both to Galatians and to the Gospel of John.

In Galatians, Paul was dealing with believers for whom Jesus' death had not changed their perception of what makes Israel, Israel. For them there had been no lessening in the authority of Israel's law, with its demand for righteousness. So Paul appealed to Jesus' crucifixion as terminating that authority.[12] Jesus' death for others had made it impossible to preserve among his followers any distinction between Jew and Gentile, male and female, master and slave (Gal. 3:28). Paul located the only source of life in the triple crucifixion: by the cross of our Lord Jesus Christ, he wrote, "the world has been crucified to me and I have been crucified to the world" (Gal. 6:14, author's translation). All three of those crucifixions took place at the same moment, and at that moment life began for all three.

In the Gospel of John, disciples stood on the boundary between two solidarities: "the world" composed of their persecutors and "the peace" of those sharing Jesus' victory over that world.[13]

> "I have told you all this so that you may receive my peace. As long as you are in the world you will be persecuted. But take heart. I have conquered the world." (John 16:33, author's translation)

Victory over the world of persecutors was victory over the maximum penalty that world could inflict—death. Martyrdom made Christians aware of the truth of the Matabele proverb: "Death . . . knows no kings; it is its own king."[14] But they also celebrated the truth of a king who, in dying, had put that death to death. That paradoxical phrase was designed to fuse two related but distinct connotations of the term *death*. One death had been put to death by another because it had lost its power to intimidate and threaten; it no longer held jurisdiction over the dead and the living. In the language of the Apocalypse, the victory of one dead man had demonstrated his power to cast Death and Hades into the lake of fire (Rev. 20:14).

This paradox may mark the sharpest contrast between two baselines of thought: one defines Jesus' death in the obviously accurate way, Jesus "breathed his last" (Luke 23:46); the other defines what took place on Golgotha in terms of putting death to death. The second baseline accords a limited place to the first, for it knows full well the actuality of martyrdom. But the first cannot accord priority to the second and remain the same. At stake is not the actuality of one death, but the credibility of the death of that death.[15]

This apparent linguistic confusion may have been what prompted the prophet John to distinguish between a first and a second death. In his apocalyptic lexicon, the first death (with its twin, the first resurrection) referred to "those who had been beheaded for their testimony to Jesus and for the word of God" (Rev. 20:4–6). Nothing could belie the actuality of such a death. That first death was part and parcel of the first heaven and earth. But the prophet also saw the actuality of Jesus' victory, which signaled the advent of the new heaven and earth, in which the first death ceased to exist.

This survey by no means exhausts the images of dying to be found in the Bible. One may recall, for example, the two pivotal announcements in the parable of the Prodigal Son: "this my son was dead, and is alive again;" . . . "this your brother was dead, and is alive" (Luke 15:24, 32). Is this death nothing more than sentimental hyperbole, or should it be taken with full seriousness? Only the latter option gives to the parable its intended force.

Then there is the familiar declaration, which is seldom treated with due respect: "We have passed out of death into life because we love the brethren. Whoever does not love dwells in death" (1 John 3:14, author's translation). Elsewhere the measure of such love is the act of dying for another. And we should not overlook the degree to which that act represents a final victory over the fear of death. Nor should we ignore the force of the antithetical declaration: "Anyone who hates his brother is a murderer, and you know that no murderer has eternal life dwelling in him" (1 John 3:15, author's translation). This equation of murder = hatred = death echoes a similar equation in the Sermon on the Mount (Matt. 5:21–22). Early Christian writers did not view acts of love or hatred as isolated decisions made by an individual alone. Just as the murder of Jesus continued the chain that began with the murder of Abel (Heb. 12:24), so the inner attitude of the Christian disclosed his relationship to the same chain.

What is an interpreter to do with such a kaleidoscope of notions? The survey is far from complete, but I have perhaps said enough to indicate the dimensions of the problem. Only an imaginative use of prepositions and verbs can distinguish the various kinds of dying and living. The kinds are so many that it is quite impossible to reduce all the references to a single standard definition of the noun. The metaphorical complexity is too great to be reduced to literal simplicity. But it is equally impossible to discount all the figures of speech as if they were nothing more than innocuous platitudes. Their anchorage in the death of Jesus and their linkage to the martyrdom of his followers prevent us from doing such violence to the language of faith. It would be an evasion and a distortion of their testimonies to suggest that the apostles and the prophets were dealing with imaginary rather than actual forms of dying.

It is probably true that in thinking about death all of us begin from a particular baseline, some conscious or subconscious definition that we share to some degree with our peers. And we tend to shape all ideas into some kind of conformity with that definition. Conversations with others are fruitful to the degree that this baseline is shared with them. When the thinking of two conversational partners starts from different premises, the conversation often proves fruitless, even antagonistic. At some point each must make an effort to adopt the other's baseline, at least for the time being. If we, then, want to grasp the perspectives that characterize the New Testament, we may well return to the Pauline text already cited and examine its structure more closely.

a   The death he died he died to sin, once for all,
b′ but the life he lives he lives to God.
c   So you also must consider yourselves dead to sin
d   and alive to God in Christ Jesus. (Rom. 6:10–11)

The first two lines, *a* and *b*, are interdependent definitions of a very specific concept of death and life. Dying to sin is the measure of being alive to God; the two are embodied in the same choice and the same action. The implied alternatives are these: either dying to sin and being alive to God, or dying to God and being alive to sin. Sin and God are mutually exclusive objects of allegiance. And, as we have seen, other nouns may be substituted for sin in this equation: dying to the law, to the world, to the self, to the devil, to the fear of death. In all these equations, the little preposition *to* is decisive. Among the various kinds of death, priority is given to this relationship to God, which is simultaneously a relationship to these competitors for loyalty.

The last two lines, *c* and *d*, also indicate the interdependence of this death and this life, as well as their decisive importance. However, the fourth line, *d*, adds a new detail when we compare it with its parallel in line *b*. Only "in Christ Jesus" do believers come alive to God. Only through believing in his dying-life, only through union with him, are they enabled to comprehend the pattern of thought and to adopt the pattern of action. Both patterns are disclosed in the Passion story. That story, precisely as a story of real events, becomes the baseline of Christian thought and action. Priority lies there.

As we read the New Testament and as we listen to music that interprets it, we should constantly recognize this baseline. That is, of course, easier to say than to do. However, we are not the first readers to encounter that difficulty; the earliest Christians were the first to learn how hard it is to exchange one set of ideas about death for another. In this they needed the help of the apostles and the prophets to whom the risen Christ had appeared and whom he had commissioned to be his messengers. Through the Holy Spirit they had received the assignment of revealing the mysteries of God's presence in the dying and rising of Jesus, of God's judgment and forgiveness of sin, and of the victory of good over evil. This gift of the Spirit included power to penetrate the secrets of human hearts and to locate there the suppressed fears of death in order to provide emancipation from those fears (Heb. 2:14–18).[16]

These prophetic messengers were the authoritative leaders of the early congregations. They fully recognized that their proclamation involved a great mystery, "Listen, I am telling you a mystery" (1 Cor. 15:51, author's translation). As the leaders of worship in the congregations, they shared this mystery—the hidden but real presence of the living Lord—with all the worshipers. This mystery illuminated their reading of the Scriptures, their leading in prayers, their celebration of the sacraments, their oral prophesying. They provided leadership not least in singing from a wide repertoire of "psalms, hymns and spiritual songs."[17] They discovered in music a highly effective way by which a congregation could rejoice in its new existence as God's people. It is true that most of their oral prophecies and most of their hymns have disappeared, yet fragments of both punctuate the literature.

It is no accident that the book that comes closest to a transcript of oral prophecy—the book of Revelation—should comprise the largest collection of poetic and hymnic materials. Unfortunately, no musical scores have survived; indeed, the melodies may have been quite spontaneous. Nevertheless there did survive in this document the texts of various amens and alleluias that were sung in praise of "the Lamb that was slain."

> "You are worthy to take the scroll
>   and to open its seals
> for you were slain and by your blood
> you ransomed for God saints
> from every tribe and language and people and nation;
> you have made them to be a kingdom,
>   priests to our God,
> and they shall reign on earth." (Rev. 5:9–10, author's translation)

I am convinced that it was the prophets who were the first leaders of music in the early church and that it was they, including John, who were the first to set the Passion story to music. Their anthems celebrated the life that was shared with all those who "washed their robes and made them white in the blood of the Lamb" (Rev. 7:14).

> "They are before the throne of God
> and worship him day and night in his temple;
> he who sits on the throne will shelter them
>   with his presence,
> for the Lamb in the midst of the throne
>   will be their shepherd,
> he will guide them to springs
>   of the water of life." (Rev. 7:15, 17, author's translation)

These two hymns, among many others in this book of prophecy, indicate clearly that singing was a wholly natural way for Christians to think about death and life. Music was one of the earliest modes of theological reflection on what had happened in the mission of Jesus and on what was continuing to happen in the mission of the church. I think of the prophets as the composers of Spirit-inspired songs to celebrate death and life.[18]

The important role of these songs comes to the surface in the letter to the Colossians (3:1–17). In this passage, note the sequence of thought as it moves toward a climax:

Verse	Quotation (Author's translation)	Comment
3	you have died	the glance backward
3	your life is hidden with Christ in God	the present home
4	when Christ, our true life, appears	the future horizon
5	therefore put to death	breaking loose from the past
12	therefore put on	taking full advantage of the present
15	let the peace of Christ rule	accepting new government
16	let the word of Christ dwell in you	a new center of gravity

Then follows a sign that this whole transformation has been made possible by the death and life of Christ:

> sing psalms and hymns and spiritual songs with thankfulness in your hearts to God. (Col. 3:16)

Such a text indicates quite clearly that the music embraced the whole range of thoughts and feelings that had been released by the Holy Spirit. It suggests how natural it was for gratitude to find expression in alleluias. For these singers, setting to music the death of Jesus was a way of setting his life to music, and theirs as well.

We should not be surprised that charismatic leaders encouraged such spiritual singing within their congregations. Music is a way of telling a story and of inviting singers to accept a role in that story. Music can articulate the rich subtleties experienced in suffering and joy. It is a language native to exiles returning to their native land, the best medium for expressing gratitude so intense as to explode in glorias. It releases a wider spectrum of emotions than can be released by confessional formulas or historical reconstructions. It evokes the sense of mystery that surrounds such homespun words as *death* and *life*. It uses sounds as a band of communication with the encompassing Silence.

Composers have, through the ages, been aware of all this; they must be, for they are primary interpreters of the text of personal and social experience. They become even more aware when they take as their text the awesome experience of death and life, and still more aware when that text is the Passion story.

JOHANN SEBASTIAN BACH

St. Matthew Passion

THE PASSION-MUSIC, ACCORDING TO MATTHEW

Johann Sebastian Bach

Christian Friedrich Henrici (Picander)
Translated by Thomas Dunn

PART I

Die Tochter Zion und die Gläubigen
Aria.

The Daughter of Zion and the Faithful
Aria.

Kommt, ihr Töchter, helft mir klagen. [1]
Sehet! **G.** *Wen?* **Z.** *den Bräutigam.*

Come, ye daughters, join my weeping.
Look! **F.** At whom? **Z.** The Bridegroom see.

Seht ihn: **G.** *Wie?* **Z.** *als wie ein Lamm.*

See him: **F.** How? **Z.** A Lamb is he.

Choral.

Chorale.

O Lamm Gottes, unschuldig
Am Stamm des Kreuzes geschlachtet.
Sehet! **G.** *Was?* **Z.** *Seht die Geduld.*
Allzeit erfunden geduldig,
Wiewohl du warest verachtet,
Seht: **G.** *Wohin?* **Z.** *auf unsre Schuld:*
Alle Sund hast du getragen,
Sonst müssten wir verzagen,
Sehet ihn aus Lieb und Huld
Holz zum Kreuze selber tragen.
Erbarm dich unser, o Jesu!
Da Capo.

O Lamb of God, not guilty,
Upon the Cross thou art slaughtered:
Look! **F.** At what? **Z.** His patience see.
Forever wast thou patient
E'en when thou wast despised.
Look! **F.** On what? **Z.** Look on our guilt.
All sins for us thou barest,
Else were we in despair.
See how he, through love and grace
Wood and Cross himself did bear.
Take pity on us, Jesus!
Da Capo.

The Rulers' Conspiracy

Da Jesus diese Rede vollendet [2]
hatte, sprach er zu seinen Jüngern:
"Ihr wisset, dass nach zweien Tagen
Ostern wird, und des Menschen Sohn
wird überantwortet werden, dass er
gekreuziget werde."

When Jesus had finished all these sayings, he said unto his disciples, Ye know that after two days is the passover, and the Son of man is betrayed to be crucified.

Choral.

Chorale.

Herzliebster Jesu, was hast du [3]
verbrochen,

Beloved Jesu, what crime hast thou committed,

Movements in chapter text refer to the C.F. Peters' vocal score; bracketed numbers in libretto parallel the Peters' movements.

Dass man ein solch scharf Urteil hat
gesprochen?
Was ist die Schuld, in was für
Missetaten
Bist du geraten?

[4] That such hard sentence hath been
passed against thee?
What is the crime: what is the evil-
doing
With which they charge thee?

Da versammelten sich die Hohenpriester und Schriftgelehrten, und die
Aeltesten im Volk, in dem Palast des
Hohenpriesters, der da hiess Caiphas;
und hielten Rat, wie sie Jesum mit
Listen griffen und töteten. Sie
sprachen aber: "Ja nicht auf das Fest,
auf dass nicht ein Aufruhr werde im
Volk."

[4] Then assembled together the chief
priests, and the scribes, and the elders
of the people, unto the palace of the
high priest, who was called Caiaphas,
and consulted that they might take Je-
[5] sus by subtilty, and kill him. But they
said, Not on the feast day, lest there
be an uproar among the people.

Jesus' Anointing for Death

Da nun Jesus war zu Bethanien,
im Hause Simonis des Aussätzigen,
trat zu ihm ein Weib, das hatte ein
Glas mit köstlichem Wasser, und goss
es auf sein Haupt, da er zu Tische
sass. Da das seine Jünger sahen, wurden sie unwillig und sprachen:
"Wozu dienet dieser Unrat? Dieses
Wasser hätte mögen teuer verkauft,
und den Armen gegeben werden."
Da das Jesus merkete, sprach er zu
ihnen: "Was bekümmert ihr das Weib?
Sie hat ein gut Werk an mir getan!
Ihr habet allezeit Arme bei euch, mich
aber habt ihr nicht allezeit Arme bei
euch, mich aber habt ihr nicht allezeit.
Dass sie dies Wasser hat auf meinen
Leib gegossen, hat sie getan, dass
man mich begraben wird. Wahrlich
ich sage euch: Wo dies Evangelium
geprediget wird in der ganzen Welt,
da wird man auch sagen zu ihrem
Gedächtnis, was sie getan hat."

[6] Now when Jesus was in Bethany,
in the house of Simon the leper,
there came unto him a woman having an alabaster box of very precious
ointment, and poured it on his head,
as he sat at meat. But when his disciples saw it, they had indignation,
[7] saying, To what purpose is this waste?
For this ointment might have been
sold for much, and given to the poor.
When Jesus understood it, he said
[8] unto them. Why trouble ye the
woman? for she hath wrought a good
work upon me. For ye have the poor
always with you; but me ye have not
always. For in that she hath poured
this ointment on my body, she did it
for my burial. Verily I say unto you,
Wheresoever this gospel shall be
preached in the whole world, there
shall also this, that this woman hath
done, be told for a memorial of her.

Recit.

Du lieber Heiland du,
Wenn deine Jünger töricht streiten,
Dass dieses fromme Weib
Mit Salben deinen Leib
Zum Grabe will bereiten:
So lasse mir inzwischen zu,
Von meiner Augen Tränenflüssen
Ein Wasser auf dein Haupt zu giessen.

Recit.

[9] Beloved Saviour, thou,
When thy disciples foolish argue
Against this woman's gift
Of ointment to prepare
Thy body to be buried,
Do grant me leave meanwhile on thee
My overflowing flood of weeping
To pour, as ointment for anointing.

Aria.

Buss und Reu
  Knirscht das Sündenherz entzwei,
  Dass die Tropfen meiner Zähren
  Angenehme Spezerei,
  Treuer Jesu, dir gebären.
    Da Capo.

Aria.

[10] Penitence
        Tears my sinning heart in two.
        Let the teardrops of my weeping
        Soothing spices ever be,
        Beloved Jesu, offered thee.
          Da Capo.

The Covenant of Betrayal

Da ging hin der Zwölfen einer, mit [11]
Namen Judas Ischarioth, zu den
Hohenpriestern, und sprach: "Was
wollt ihr mir geben? Ich will ihn euch
verratern." Und sie boten ihm dreissig
Silberlinge. Und von dem an suchte
er Gelegenheit, dass er ihn verriete.

Then one of the twelve, called Judas Iscariot, went unto the chief
priests, and said unto them, What
will ye give me, and I will deliver
him unto you? And they covenanted
with him for thirty pieces of silver.
And from that time he sought opportunity to betray him.

Aria.

Blute nur, du liebes Herz!
Ach, ein Kind, das du erzogen,
Das an deiner Brust gesogen,
Droht den Pfleger zu ermorden,
Denn es ist zur Schlange worden.
Blute nur, du liebes Herz.

Aria.

[12]   Suffer this, beloved heart!
        Ah, a child, whom thou hast cherished
        And ever in thy breast hath nurtured,
        Threatens murder to his guardian,
        Like a deadly snake becoming.
        Suffer this, beloved heart!

The Eating of the Passover

Aber am ersten Tage der süssen [13]
Brot, traten die Jünger zu Jesu, und
sprachen zu ihm: "Wo willst du, dass [14]
wir dir bereiten das Osterlamm zu es-
sen?" Er sprach: "Gehet hin in die [15]
Stadt zu Einem, und sprecht zu ihm:
Der Meister lässt dir sagen: 'Meine
Zeit ist hie, ich will bei dir die Ostern
halten mit meinen Jüngern.'" Und
die Jünger täten, wie ihnen Jesus be-
fohlen hatte, und bereiteten das
Osterlamm.

Und am Abend satzte er sich zu
Tische mit den Zwölfen; und da sie
assen, sprach er: "Wahrlich, ich sage
euch: Einer unter euch wird mich ver-
raten." Und sie wurden sehr betrübt,
und huben an, ein Jeglicher unter
ihnen, und sagten zu ihm: "Herr, bin
ich's?"

Now the first day of the feast of unleavened bread the disciples came to
Jesus, saying unto him, Where wilt
thou that we prepare for thee to eat
the passover? And he said, Go into
the city to such a man, and say unto
him, The Master saith, My time is at
hand; I will keep the passover at thy
house with my disciples. And the disciples did as Jesus appointed them;
and they made ready the passover.

Now when the even was come, he
sat down with the twelve. And as they
did eat, he said, Verily I say unto
you, that one of you shall betray me.
And they were exceeding sorrowful,
and began every one of them to say
unto him, Lord, is it I?

Choral.

Ich bin's, ich sollte büssen,   [16]
An Händen und an Füssen
Gebunden in der Höll.'
Die Geisseln und die Banden,
Und was du ausgestanden,
Das hat verdienet meine Seel.'

Er antwortete und sprach: "Der mit [17]
der Hand mit mir in die Schüssel
tauchet, der wird mich verraten. Des
Menschen Sohn gehet zwar dahin,
wie von ihm geschrieben stehet: doch
wehe dem Menschen, durch welchen
des Menschen Sohn verraten wird. Es
wäre ihm besser, dass derselbige
Mensch noch nie geboren wäre." Da
antwortete Judas, der ihn verriet und
sprach: "Bin ich's, Rabbi?" Er sprach
zu ihm: "Du sagest's."

Chorale.

It is I who should do penance,
And hand and foot be bound
Repentently in Hell.
The whipping and the scourging,
And all that thou hast borne
Are punishments my soul hath earned.

He answered and said, He that dip-
peth his hand with me in the dish,
the same shall betray me. The Son of
man goeth as it is written of him: but
woe unto that man by whom the Son
of man is betrayed! it had been good
for that man if he had not been born.
Then Judas, which betrayed him, answered and said, Master, is it I? He
said unto him. Thou hast said.

The Institution of the Blessed Sacrament

Da sie aber assen, nahm Jesus das
Brot, dankete und brach's, und gab's
den Jüngern und sprach: "Nehmet, es-
set, das ist mein Leib." Und er nahm
den Kelch, und dankete, gab ihnen
den, und sprach: "Trinket alle daraus;
das ist mein Blut des neuen Testa-
ments, welches vergossen wird für
Viele, zur Vergebung der Sünden. Ich
sage euch: ich werde von nun an nicht
mehr von diesem Gewächs des Wein-
stocks trinken, bis an den Tag, da ich's
neu trinken werde mit euch in meines
Vaters Reich."

And as they were eating, Jesus took
bread, and blessed it, and brake it,
and gave it to the disciples, and said.
Take, eat; this is my body. And he
took the cup, and gave thanks, and
gave it to them, saying, Drink ye all
of it: for this is my blood of the new
testament, which is shed for many for
the remission of sins. But I say unto
you, I will not drink henceforth of
this fruit of the vine, until that day
when I drink it new with you in my
Father's kingdom.

Recit.

Wiewohl mein Herz in Tränen   [18]
   schwimmt,
Das Jesus von mir Abschied nimmt,
So macht mich doch sein Testament
   erfreut;
Sein Fleisch und Blut, o Kostbarkeit!
Vermacht er mir in meine Hände,
Wie er es auf der Welt mit denen
   Seinen
Nicht böse können meinen,
So liebt er sie bis an das Ende.

Recit.

Although my heart now swims in
   tears
That Jesus must from me depart,
Yet doth his testament make me
   rejoice:
His flesh and blood, O priceless gifts,
Into my hands he here bequeathes.
As he, when in this world amidst his
   own,
No evil did intend,
Still loves he them unto the end.

Aria.   *Aria.*

Ich will dir mein Herze schenken,   [19]   I would offer thee my heart;
  Senke dich, mein Heil, hinein.   Fill it, my Salvation.
Ich will mich in dir versenken;   I would lose myself in thee;
  Ist dir gleich die Welt zu klein,   If to thee the world seems small,
  Ei! so sollst du mir allein   Thou thyself alone to me
  Mehr als Welt und Himmel sein   Art more than earth or heaven.
                          Da Capo.   *Da Capo.*

The Prophecy of Denial

Und da sie den Lobgesang ge- [20]   And when they had sung an
sprochen hatten, gingen sie hinaus an   hymn, they went out into the mount
den Oelberg. Da sprach Jesus zu ih-   of Olives. Then saith Jesus unto
nen: "In dieser Nacht werdet ihr euch   them, All ye shall be offended be-
alle ärgern an mir. Denn es stehet ge-   cause of me this night: for it is written
schrieben: Ich werde den Hirten   I will smite the shepherd, and the
schlagen, und die Schafe der Herde   sheep of the flock shall be scattered
werden sich zerstreuen. Wann ich   abroad. But after I am risen again, I
aber auferstehe, will ich vor euch hin- will go before you into Galilee.
gehen in Galiläam."

Choral.   *Chorale.*

Erkenne mich, mein Hüter,   [21]   Thou know'st me, O my guardian;
Mein Hirte, nimm mich an.   My shepherd, keep thou me.
Von dir, Quell aller Güter,   By thee, source of all goodness,
Ist mir viel Gut's getan.   Such good things have been given.
Dein Mund hat mich gelabet   Thy mouth hath oft refreshed me
Mit Milch und süsser Kost,   With milk, unleavened bread;
Dein Geist hat mich begabet   Thy spirit ever gave me
Mit mancher Himmelslust.   The many joys of Heaven.

Petrus aber antwortete, und sprach [22]   Peter answered and said unto him.
zu ihm: "Wenn sie auch alle sich an   Though all men shall be offended be-
dir ärgerten, so will ich doch mich   cause of thee, yet will I never be of-
nimmermehr ärgern." Jesus sprach zu   fended. Jesus said unto him, Verily I
ihm: "Wahrlich, ich sage dir: in dieser say unto thee, That this night, before
Nacht, ehe der Hahn krähet, wirst du   the cock crow, thou shalt deny me
mich dreimal verleugnen." Petrus   thrice. Peter said unto him, Though
sprach zu ihm: "Und wenn ich mit dir   I should die with thee, yet will I not
sterben müsste, so will ich dich nicht   deny thee. Likewise also said all the
verleugnen." Desgleichen sagten auch   disciples.
alle Jünger.

Choral.   *Chorale.*

Ich will hier bei dir stehen;   [23]   I would stay here beside thee:
Verachte mich doch nicht!   O cast me not away.
Von dir will ich nicht gehen,   From thee I will not turn me,
Wenn dir dein Herze bricht.   E'en when thy heart will break.
Wenn dein Herz wird erblassen   When thy heart fades in pallor

Im letzten Todesstoss,   Of death's last firm embrace,
Alsdann will ich dich fassen   Then would I clasp thee to me,
In meinen Arm und Schoss.   With arms and heart embrace.

Christ's Agony in the Garden

Da kam Jesus mit ihnen zu einem [24]   Then cometh Jesus with them
Hofe, der hiess Gethsemane, und   unto a place called Gethsemane, and
sprach zu seinen Jüngern: "Setzet   saith unto the disciples, Sit ye here,
euch hie, bis dass ich dorthingehe,   while I go and pray yonder. And he
und bete." Und nahm zu sich Petrum   took with him Peter and the two sons
und die zween Söhne Zebedäi und   of Zebedee, and began to be sorrow-
fing an zu trauern und zu zagen. Da   ful and very heavy. Then saith he
sprach Jesus zu ihnen: "Meine Seele   unto them, My soul is exceeding sor-
ist betrübt bis an den Tod: bleibet   rowful, even unto death: tarry ye
hier, und wachet mit mir."   here, and watch with me.

Zion und die Gläubigen.   *Zion and the Faithful.*
Recit.   *Recit.*

Z. *O Schmerz!*   [25]   **Z.** O pain!
   Hier zittert das gequälte Herz;   Here trembles his sore-troubled heart;
   Wie sinkt es hin! wie bleicht sein   It sinks away! how pale his
   Angesicht!   countenance!

Chor der Gläubigen.   *Chorus of the Faithful.*

G. *Was ist die Ursach' aller solcher*   **F.** What is the reason for such awful
   Plagen?   torment?
Z. *Der Richter führt ihn vor Gericht,* **Z.** The Judge now leads him to be judged,
   Da ist kein Trost, kein Helfer   There is no comfort nor helper
   nicht.   there.
G. *Ach, meine Sünden haben dich*   **F.** Alas, my sins are those which
   geschlagen.   have thee smitten.
Z. *Er leidet alle Höllenqualen,*   **Z.** He suffers all Hell's bitter torments,
   Er soll für fremden Raub   And is as strangers' ransom counted.
   bezahlen.
G. *Ich, ach Herr Jesu, habe dies*   **F.** I, O Lord Jesu, I alone am guilty
   verschuldet,
   Was du erduldet!   Of what you suffer.
Z. *Ach könnte meine Liebe dir,*   **Z.** O might my love for thee, my Lord,
   Mein Heil, dein Zittern und dein   But ease thy fear and trembling,
   Zagen,
   Vermindern oder helfen tragen,   And lessen them to help thee bear them,
   Wie gerne blieb' ich hier!   How gladly would I stay!

Aria à Duetto.   *Aria à Duetto.*

Z. *Ich will bei meinem Jesu wachen,* [26] **Z.** I would keep watch with Jesus,
G. *So schlafen unsere Sünden ein.*   **F.** And so our sins fall fast asleep.
Z. *Meinen Tod*   **Z.** For my death
   Büsset seiner Seelen Not.   His pain of soul atones,
   Sein Trauern machet mich voll Freuden,   His sorrow makes joy full for me.

G. *Drum muss uns sein verdienstlich
  Leiden
  Recht bitter und doch süsse sein.*
  Da Capo.

F. Therefore his righteous suffering
  must
  Be bitter for us, but still sweet.
  Da Capo.

*Und ging hin ein wenig, fiel nieder
auf sein Angesicht, und betete, und
sprach: "Mein Vater, ist's möglich, so
gehe dieser Kelch von mir; doch nicht
wie ich will, sondern wie du willst."*

[27] And he went a little farther, and fell
on his face, and prayed, saying, O my
Father, if it be possible, let this cup
pass from me: nevertheless not as I
will, but as thou wilt.

Recit.

Recit.

*Der Heiland fällt vor seinem Vater
  nieder,
Dadurch erhebt er mich und alle
Von unserem Falle
Hinauf zu Gottes Gnade wieder.
Er ist bereit,
Den Kelch des Todes Bitterkeit zu
  trinken,
In welchen Sünden dieser Welt
Gegossen sind, und hässlich stinken,
Weil es dem lieben Gott gefallt.*

[28] The Saviour, falling down before his
  Father,
Thereby hath lifted me and others,
Having fallen,
Back up to God's good grace again.
He is prepared
To drink the cup of bitterness of
  dying.
In which the sins throughout the world
Have all been poured, and stink of evil.
So to the loving Lord it falls.

Aria.

Aria.

*Gerne will ich mich bequemen,
Kreuz und Becher anzunehmen,
Trink ich doch dem Heiland nach.
  Denn sein Mund,
Der mit Milch und Honig fliesset,
  Hat den Grund
Und des Leidens herbe Schmach
Durch den ersten Trunk versüsset.*
  Da Capo.

[29] Gladly would I be accepting
Cross and cup with joy receiving,
Drinking as my Saviour drinks.
  For his mouth,
Which with milk and honey floweth,
  All the dregs
And the bitter taste of pain,
By his drinking first, hath sweetened.
  Da Capo.

*Und er kam zu seinen Jüngern,
und fand sie schlafend, und sprach zu
ihnen: "Könnet ihr denn nicht eine
Stunde mit mir wachen? Wachet und
betet, dass ihr nicht in Anfechtung
fallet. Der Geist ist willig, aber das
Fleisch ist schwach." Zum andern
Mal ging er hin, betete und sprach:
"Mein Vater, ist's nicht möglich, dass
dieser Kelch von mir gehe, ich trinke
ihn denn, so geschehe dein Wille."*

[30] And he cometh unto the disciples,
and findeth them asleep, and saith
unto Peter, What, could ye not watch
with me one hour? Watch and pray,
that ye enter not into temptation: the
spirit indeed is willing, but the flesh
is weak. He went away again the second time, and prayed, saying, O my
Father, if this cup may not pass away
from me, except I drink it, thy will be
done.

Choral.

Chorale.

*Was mein Gott will, das gescheh' allzeit,
Sein Will' der ist der beste;*

[31] What my God wills will ever be;
His will is best forever.

Zu helfen den'n er ist bereit,	To help them who believe on him
Die an ihn glauben feste.	He is forever ready.
Er hilft aus Not,	He helps in need,
Der fromme Gott,	The righteous God,
Und züchtiget mit Massen.	And chastiseth in mercy.
Wer Gott vertraut,	Who trusts in God
Fest auf ihn baut,	and builds on him
Den will er nicht verlassen.	Will never be forsaken.

Und er kam und fand sie aber [32] *schlafend, und ihre Augen waren voll Schlafs. Und er liess sie, und ging abermals hin, und betete zum dritten Mal, und redete dieselbigen Worte. Da kam er zu seinen Jüngern, und sprach zu ihnen: "Ach! Wollt ihr nun schlafen und ruhen? Siehe, die Stunde ist hie, dass des Menschen Sohn in der Sünder Hände überantwortet wird. Stehet auf, lasset uns gehen; siehe, er ist da, der mich verrät."*

And he came and found them asleep again: for their eyes were heavy. And he left them, and went away again, and prayed the third time, saying the same words. Then cometh he to his disciples, and saith unto them, Sleep on now, and take your rest: behold, the hour is at hand, and the Son of man is betrayed into the hands of sinners. Rise, let us be going: behold, he is at hand that doth betray me.

The Betrayal and Arrest

Und als er noch redete, siehe, da kam Judas, der Zwölfen einer, und mit ihm eine grosse Schar, mit Schwerten und mit Stangen, von den Hohenpriestern und Aeltesten des Volks. Und der Verräter hatte ihnen ein Zeichen gegeben, und gesagt: "Welchen ich küssen werde, der ist's, den greifet." Und alsbald trat er zu Jesum und sprach: "Gegrüsset sei'st du, Rabbi!" Und küssete ihn. Jesus aber sprach zu ihm: "Mein Freund! warum bist du kommen?" Da traten sie hinzu, und legten die Hände an Jesum, und griffen ihn.

And while he yet spake, lo, Judas, one of the twelve, came, and with him a great multitude with swords and staves, from the chief priests and elders of the people. Now he that betrayed him gave them a sign, saying, Whomsoever I shall kiss, that same is he: hold him fast. And forthwith he came to Jesus, and said, Hail, master: and kissed him. And Jesus said unto him, Friend, wherefore art thou come? Then came they, and laid hands on Jesus, and took him.

Zion und die Gläubigen.
Aria à 1.

Z. *So ist mein Jesus nun gefangen,*
G. *Lasst ihn! haltet! bindet nicht!*
Z. *Mond und Licht,*
   Ist vor Schmerzen untergangen,
   Weil mein Jesus ist gefangen.
G. *Lasst ihn! haltet! bindet nicht!*
Z. *Sie führen ihn, er ist gebunden.*

Zion and the Faithful.
Aria à 1.

[33] Z. See how my Jesus hath been taken,
F. Leave him! Stop! bind him not!
Z. Moon and light
   For the shame have hid their faces,
   Since my Jesus hath been taken.
F. Leave him! Stop! bind him not!
Z. They lead him out; they have
   bound him.

Aria à 2.

Sind Blitze, sind Donner in
Wolken verschwunden!
Eröffne den feurigen Abgrund, o
Hölle!
Zertrümmre, verderbe,
verschlinge, zerschelle
Mit plötzlicher Wut
Den falschen Verräter, das
mördrische Blut.

Und siehe, einer aus denen, die mit
Jesu waren, reckete die Hand aus,
und schlug des Hohenpriesters
Knecht, und hieb ihm ein Ohr ab. Da
sprach Jesus zu ihm: "Stecke dein
Schwert an seinen Ort; denn wer das
Schwert nimmt, der soll durchs
Schwert umkommen. Oder meinest
du, dass ich nicht könnte meinen Va-
ter bitten, dass er mir zuschickte mehr
denn zwölf Legion Engel? Wie würde
aber die Schrift erfüllet? Es muss also
gehen 'Zu der Stund' sprach Jesus zu
den Scharen: "Ihr seid ausgegangen,
als zu einem Mörder, mit Schwerten
und mit Stangen mich zu fahen; bin
ich doch täglich bei euch gesessen,
und habe gelehret im Tempel, und ihr
habt mich nicht gegriffen. Aber das ist
alles geschehen, dass erfüllet würden
die Schriften der Propheten." Da ver-
liessen ihn alle Jünger und flohen.

Choral.

O Mensch, bewein' dein' Sünde gross:
Darum Christus sein's Vaters Schoss
Aeussert, und kam auf Erden.
Von einer Jungfrau rein und zart
Für uns er hie geboren ward,
Er wollt' der Mittler werden.
Den'n Toten er das Leben gab,
Und legt' dabei, all' Krankheit ab,
Bis sich die Zeit herdrange,
Dass er für uns geopfert würd',
Trüg unsrer Sünden schwere Bürd'
Wohl an dem Kreuze lange.

Aria à 2.

The lightning and thunder in
dark clouds have vanished!
Let Hell's fiery yawning abyss
wide be opened!
And swallow him up, twist and
dash him to pieces
In frenzy most swift,
That untrue betrayer, that
murderous blood.

[34] And, behold, one of them which
were with Jesus stretched out his
hand, and drew his sword, and struck
a servant of the high priest's and
smote off his ear. Then said Jesus
unto him, Put up again thy sword
into his place: for all they that take
the sword shall perish with the sword.
Thinkest thou that I cannot now pray
to my Father, and he shall even now
give me more than twelve legions of
angels? But how then shall the scriptures be fulfilled, that thus it must
be? In the same hour said Jesus to the
multitudes, Are ye come out as
against a robber with swords and
staves for to take me? I sat daily with
you teaching in the temple, and ye
laid no hold on me. But all this was
done, that the scriptures of the prophets might be fulfilled. Then all the
disciples forsook him and fled.

Chorale.

[35] O man, bewail thy grievous sin,
For which Christ from his Father's throne
On earth was manifested,
And of a virgin, full of grace,
For all mankind he here was born
To be the mediator.
The dead he gave back life again
And sickness from men laid aside,
Until the time did warrant
That he be offered up for us,
And bear our sins' most heavy weight,
So long the Cross enduring.

PART II

Aria.	*Aria.*
Die Gläubigen, und Zion.	*The Faithful, and Zion.*

Z. *Ach! nun ist mein Jesus hin!*   [36]   **Z.** Now is my Jesus gone!
G. *Wo ist denn dein Freund*   **F.** Where hath thy beloved departed,
    hingegangen,
    O du Schönste unter den Weibern?   O thou fairest amongst all women?
Z. *Ist es möglich? Kann ich schauen?*   **Z.** Is it possible? can I bear it?
G. *Wo hat sich dein Freund*   **F.** Whither hath thy friend gone
    hingewandt?   astray?
Z. *Ach! mein Lamm in Tigerklauen!*   **Z.** Ah, my lamb in tiger's claws!
    Ach! wo ist mein Jesus hin?   Ah, where is my Jesus gone?
G. *So wollen wir mit dir ihn suchen.*   **F.** For we would go with thee to seek
                                                               him.
Z. *Was soll ich der Seele sagen?*   **Z.** What can I say to my spirit
    Wenn sie mich wird ängstlich fragen?   If it anxiously be asking,
    Ach! wo ist mein Jesus hin?   Ah, where is my Jesus gone?

The Trial Before Caiaphas

Die aber Jesum gegriffen hatten, [37]   And they that had laid hold on Je-
führeten ihn zu dem Hohen-   sus led him away to Caiaphas the
priester Caiphas dahin die Schriftge-   high priest, where the scribes and the
lehrten und Aeltesten sich versammelt   elders were assembled. But Peter fol-
hatten. Petrus aber folgete ihm nach   lowed him afar off unto the high
von ferne, bis in den Palast des Hoh-   priest's palace, and went in and sat
enpriesters; und ging hinein, und   with the servants, to see the end.
satzte sich bei den knechten, auf dass   Now the chief priests, and elders, and
er sähe, wo es hinaus wollte. Die   all the council, sought false witness
Hohenpriester aber und Aeltesten,   against Jesus, to put him to death; but
und der ganze Rat, suchten falsches   found none:
Zeugnis wider Jesum, auf dass sie ihn
töteten, und fanden keines.

Choral.	*Chorale.*

Mir hat die Welt trüglich gerich't [38]   The world has judged me treach'rously
Mit Lügen und mit falschem   With false reports and lying words,
    G'dicht,
Viel Netz und heimlich Stricken.   With nets and secret snares.
Herr, nimm mein wahr   Lord, keep me safe,
In dieser G'fahr,   From danger free;
B'hüt mich vor falschen Tücken.   From all false malice shield me.

Und wiewohl viel falsche Zeugen [39]   Yea, though many false witnesses
herzutraten, funden sie doch keins.   came, yet found they none. At the
Zuletzt traten herzu zween falsche   last came two false witnesses, and
Zeugen, und sprachen: "Er hat gesagt   said, This fellow said, I am able to
'Ich kann den Tempel Gottes ab-   destroy the temple of God, and to

brechen, und in dreien Tagen desselben bauen.' Und der Hohepriester stund auf und sprach zu ihm: "Antwortest du nichts zu dem, das diese wider dich zeugen?" Aber Jesus schwieg stille.

build it in three days. And the high priest arose, and said unto him, Answerest thou nothing? what is it which these witness against thee? But Jesus held his peace.

Recit.

Mein Jesus schweigt
Zu falschen Lügen stille,
Um uns damit zu zeigen,
Dass sein erbarmensvoller Wille
Vor uns zum Leiden sei geneigt,
Und dass wir in dergleichen Pein
Ihm sollen ähnlich sein,
Und in Verfolgung stille schweigen.

Recit.

[40] He holds his peace:
To all false lies is silent,
That he thereby may show us
How he in mercy bends his will:
For us in sorrow it inclines.
So may we when in like distress
Be ever like to him,
In persecution still be silent.

Aria.

Geduld!
Wenn mich falsche Zungen stechen.
Leid ich wider meine Schuld
Schimpf und Spott,
Ei! so mag der liebe Gott
Meines Herzens Unschuld rächen.
Da Capo.

Aria.

Forbear!
[41] E'en if lying tongues should prick me.
If I suffer through no fault
Ridicule,
Aye, then may my loving God
For my innocence avenge me.
Da Capo.

Und der Hohepriester antwortete, und sprach zu ihm: "Ich beschwöre dich bei dem lebendigen Gott, dass du uns sagest, ob du seiest Christus, der Sohn Gottes." Jesus sprach zu ihm: "Du sagest's. Doch sage ich euch, von nun an wird's geschehen, dass ihr sehen werdet des Menschen Sohn sitzen zur Rechten der Kraft, und kommen in den Wolken des Himmels." Da zerriss der Hohepriester seine Kleider, und sprach: "Er hat Gott gelästert; was dürfen wir weiter Zeugnis? Siehe, jetzt habt ihr seine Gotteslästerung gehöret. Was dünket euch?" Sie antworteten, und sprachen: "Er ist des Todes schuldig!" Da speieten sie aus in sein Angesicht, und schlugen ihn mit Fäusten. Etliche aber schlugen ihn ins Angesicht und sprachen: "Weissage uns Christe, wer ist's der dich schlug?"

[42] And the high priest answered and said unto him, I adjure thee by the living God, that thou tell us whether thou be the Christ, the Son of God. Jesus saith unto him, Thou hast said: nevertheless I say unto you. Hereafter shall ye see the Son of man sitting on the right hand of power, and coming in the clouds of heaven. Then the high priest rent his clothes, saying, He hath spoken blasphemy; what further need have we for witnesses? behold, now ye have heard his blasphemy. What think ye? They answered and said, He is guilty of death.

[43] Then did they spit in his face, and buffeted him; and others smote him with the palms of their hands, saying, Prophesy unto us, thou Christ, Who is he that smote thee?

Choral.

Wer hat dich so geschlagen,
Mein Heil, und dich mit Plagen
So übel zugericht'?
Du bist ja nicht ein Sünder,
Wie wir und unsre Kinder;
Von Missetaten weisst du nicht.

[44]

Chorale.

Who was it, Lord, that struck thee,
And with such torments taunted,
So foully judging thee?
Thou never wert a sinner
Like us and like our children;
Of evil-doing know'st thou naught.

Peter's Denial

Petrus aber sass draussen im Pal- [45]
ast; und es trat zu ihm eine Magd
und sprach: "Und du warest auch mit
dem Jesu aus Galiläa." Er leugnete
aber vor ihnen allen und sprach: "Ich
weiss nicht, was du sagest." Als er
aber zur Tür hinausging, sahe ihn
eine andere, und sprach zu denen, die
da waren: "Dieser war auch mit dem
Jesu von Nazareth." Und er leugnete
abermal, und schwur dazu: "Ich
kenne des Menschen nicht." Und über
eine kleine Weile traten hinzu, die da
standen, und sprachen zu Petro:
"Wahrlich, du bist auch einer von
denen, denn deine Sprache verrät
dich." Da hub er an sich zu verfluchen [46]
und zu schwören: "Ich kenne des
Menschen nicht!" Und alsbald krä-
hete der Hahn. Da dachte Petrus an
die Worte Jesu, da er zu ihm sagte:
"Ehe der Hahn krähen wird, wirst du
mich dreimal verleugnen." Und ging
heraus, und weinete bitterlich.

Now Peter sat without in the palace: and a damsel came unto him
saying, Thou also wast with Jesus of
Galilee. But he denied before them
all, saying, I know not what thou sayest. And when he was gone out into
the porch, another maid saw him,
and said unto them that were there,
This fellow was also with Jesus of
Nazareth. And again he denied with
an oath, I do not know the man. And
after a while came unto him they that
stood by, and said to Peter, Surely
thou also art one of them; for thy
speech betrayeth thee.

Then began he to curse and to
swear, saying, I know not the man.
And immediately the cock crew. And
Peter remembered the word of Jesus,
which said unto him, Before the cock
crow, thou shalt deny me thrice. And
he went out, and wept bitterly.

Aria.

Erbarme dich,
Mein Gott, um meiner Zähren willen.
Schaue hier,
Herz und Auge weint vor dir
Bitterlich.
Erbarme dich,
Mein Gott, um meiner Zähren willen.

[47]

Aria.

Have pity, Lord,
My God, have pity on my crying.
Look on me,
Heart and eyes now weep for thee
Bitterly.
Have pity, Lord,
My God, have pity on my crying.

Choral.

Bin ich gleich von dir gewichen,
Stell' ich mich doch wieder ein;
Hat uns doch dein Sohn verglichen
Durch sein' Angst und Todespein.

[48]

Chorale.

If from thee I oft have fallen,
Place me back with thee again;
For thy Son hath reconciled us
Through the agony of death.

Ich verleug'ne nicht die Schuld,
Aber deine Gnad' und Huld
Ist viel grösser als die Sünde,
Die ich stets in mir befinde.

I cannot deny my guilt,
But thy mercy and thy grace
Are far greater than the sinning
Which I find so much within me.

Des Morgens aber hielten alle [49]
Hohenpriester und die Aeltesten des
Volks einen Rat über Jesum, dass sie
ihn töteten. Und banden ihn, führe-
ten ihn hin, und überantworteten ihn
dem Landpfleger Pontio Pilato.

When the morning was come, all
the chief priests and elders of the
people took counsel against Jesus to
put him to death: and when they had
bound him, they led him away, and
delivered him to Pontius Pilate the
governor.

Judas' Repentance and Suicide

Da das sahe Judas, der ihn verraten
hatte, dass er verdammt war zum
Tode, gereuete es ihn, und brachte her
wieder die dreissig Silberlinge den
Hohenpriestern und Aeltesten, und
sprach: "Ich habe übel getan, dass ich
unschuldig Blut verraten habe." Sie [50]
sprachen: "Was gehet uns das an? Da
siehe du zu." Und er warf die Silber-
linge in den Tempel, hub sich davon,
ging hin, und er hängete sich selbst.
Aber die Hohenpriester nahmen die
Silberlinge und sprachen: "Es taugt
nicht, dass wir sie in den Gottes-
kasten legen, denn es ist Blutgeld."

Then Judas, which had betrayed
him, when he saw that he was con-
demned, repented himself, and
brought again the thirty pieces of silver to the chief priests and elders, saying, I have sinned in that I have
betrayed the innocent blood. And
they said, What is that to us? see thou
to that. And he cast down the pieces
of silver in the temple, and departed,
and went and hanged himself. And
the chief priests took the silver pieces,
and said, It is not lawful for to put
them into the treasury, because it is
the price of blood.

Aria.   Aria.

Gebt mir meinen Jesum wieder!   [51]
  Seht, das Geld, den Mörderlohn
    Wirft euch der verlor'ne Sohn
Zu den Füssen nieder.
Gebt mir meinen Jesum wieder!

Give my Jesus back again
  See the price of murder done
    Thrown by a forsaken son
At their feet in horror
Give my Jesus back again.

Sie hielten aber einen Rat, und [52]
kauften einen Töpfers Acker darum,
zum Begräbnis der Pilger. Daher ist
derselbige Acker genennet der Blut-
acker, bis auf den heutigen Tag. Da
ist erfüllet, das gesagt ist durch den
Propheten Jeremias, da er spricht: "Sie
haben genommen dreissig Silberlinge,
damit bezahlet ward der Verkaufte,
welchen sie kauften von den Kindern
Israel; und haben sie gegeben um
einen Töpfers Acker, als mir der Herr
befohlen hat."

And they took counsel, and bought
with them the potter's field, to bury
strangers in. Wherefore that field was
called, The field of blood, unto this
day. Then was fulfilled that which
was spoken by Jeremy the prophet,
saying, And they took the thirty
pieces of silver, the price of him that
was valued, whom they of the children of Israel did value: and gave
them for the potter's field, as the Lord
appointed me.

The Trial Before Pilate

Jesus aber stand vor dem Land-
pfleger, und der Landpfleger fragte
ihn, und sprach: "Bist du der Juden
König?" Jesus aber sprach zu ihm:
"Du sagest's." Und da er verklagt
ward von den Hohenpriestern und
Aeltesten, antwortete er nichts. Da
sprach Pilatus zu ihm: "Hörest du
nicht, wie hart sie dich verklagen?"
Und er antwortete ihm nicht auf ein
Wort, also, dass sich auch der Land-
pfleger sehr verwunderte.

And Jesus stood before the governor: and the governor asked him, saying, Art thou the King of the Jews?
And Jesus said unto him, Thou sayest. And when he was accused of the
chief priests and elders, he answered
nothing. Then said Pilate unto him,
Hearest thou not how many things
they witness against thee? And he answered him to never a word; inso-
much that the governor marvelled
greatly.

Choral.

Chorale.

Befiehl du deine Wege   [53]
Und was dein Herze kränkt,
Der allertreusten Pflege
Dess, der den Himmel lenkt;
Der Wolken, Luft und Winden
Gibt Wege, Lauf und Bahn,
Der wird auch Wege finden,
Da dein Fuss gehen kann.

Commit thy path and footsteps,
And all that grieves thy heart,
To him, the faithful ruler,
Who steers the heavens course.
He gives the clouds their orbit,
The wind and air their track,
And he will set a pathway,
That thy foot go aright.

Auf das Fest hatte der Landpfleger [54]
Gewohnheit, dem Volk einen Gefang-
enen loszugeben, welchen sie wollten.
Er hatte aber zu der Zeit einen Ge-
fangenen, einen sonderlichen vor and-
ern, der hiess Barrabas. Und da sie
versammelt waren, sprach Pilatus zu
ihnen: "Welchen wollet ihr, dass ich
euch losgebe? Barrabam, oder Jesum,
von dem gesaget wird, er sei Chris-
tus." Denn er wusste wohl, dass sie
ihn aus Neid überantwortet hatten.

Now at that feast the governor was
wont to release unto the people a
prisoner, whom they would. And
they had then a notable prisoner,
called Barabbas. Therefore when
they were gathered together, Pilate
said unto them, Whom will ye that I
release unto you? Barabbas, or Jesus
which is called Christ? For he knew
that for envy they had delivered him.

Und da er auf dem Richtstuhl sass,
schikkete sein Weib zu ihm und liess
ihm sagen: "Habe du nichts zu schaff-
en mit diesem Gerechten; ich habe
heute viel erlitten im Traum von
seinetwegen." Aber die Hohenpriester
und die Aeltesten überredeten das
Volk, dass sie um Barrabam bitten
sollten, und Jesum umbrächten. Da
antwortete nun der Landpfleger und
sprach zu ihnen: "Welchen wollt ihr
unter diesen zweien, den ich euch soll

When he was set down on the
judgment seat, his wife sent unto
him, saying, Have thou nothing to do
with that just man: for I have suffered
many things this day in a dream because of him. But the chief priests
and elders persuaded the multitude
that they should ask Barabbas, and
destroy Jesus. The governor answered
and said unto them, Whether of the
twain will ye that I release unto you?
They said, Barabbas. Pilate saith unto

losgeben?" Sie sprachen: "Barrabam!"
Pilatus sprach zu ihnen: "Was soll ich
denn machen mit Jesu, von dem ge-
sagt wird, er sei Christus? Sie
sprachen alle: "Lass ihn kreuzigen.

them, What shall I do then with Jesus
which is called Christ? They all say
unto him, Let him be crucified.

Choral.

Chorale.

Wie wunderbarlich ist doch diese
 Strafe!
Der gute Hirte leidet für die Schafe;

Die Schuld bezahlt der Herre, der
 Gerechte,
Für seine Knechte!

[55] How to be pondered is this wondrous
 sentence!
The shepherd, faithful to his sheep,
 must suffer;
The price of guilt the righteous Lord
 and Master
Pays for his servant.

Der Landpfleger sagte: "Was hat er
 denn Uebels getan?"

[56] And the governor said, Why what
 evil hath he done?

Recit.

Recit.

Er hat uns allen wohl getan.
Den Blinden gab er das Gesicht,
Die Lahmen macht' er gehend;
Er sagt' uns seines Vaters Wort,
Er trieb die Teufel fort;
Betrübte hat er aufgericht't;
Er nahm die Sünder auf und an;
Sonst hat mein Jesus nichts getan.

[57] He hath done good things for us all,
A blind man he gave back his sight,
A lame man made he walk,
He told us of his Father's Word,
He drove the Devil out.
Those troubled hath he comforted,
He took upon himself our sins;
Naught else hath Jesus ever done.

Aria.

Aria.

 Aus Liebe,
Aus Liebe will mein Heiland sterben!
Von einer Sünde weiss er nichts.
Dass das ewige Verderben
 Und die Strafe des Gerichts
Nicht auf meiner Seele bliebe.
 Aus Liebe,
Aus Liebe will mein Heiland sterben!

[58] Of Love,
Of love my Saviour now would die!
 Of other sins he knoweth naught,
But that everlasting ruin,
 And the sentence of the judge
Not remain upon my soul,
 Of Love,
Of love my Saviour now would die!

Sie schrieen aber noch mehr, und
sprachen: "Lass ihn kreuzigen."
Da aber Pilatus sahe, dass er nichts
schaffete, sondern dass ein viel grösser
Getümmel ward, nahm er Wasser
und wusch die Hände vor dem Volk,
und sprach: "Ich bin unschuldig an
dem Blut dieses Gerechten, sehet ihr
zu." Da antwortete das ganze Volk,
und sprach: "Sein Blut komme über
uns und unsre Kinder."

[59] But they cried out the more, saying, Let him be crucified.
 When Pilate saw that he could pre-
vail nothing, but that rather a tumult
was made, he took water, and washed
his hands before the multitude, saying, I am innocent of the blood of
this just person: see ye to it. Then answered all the people, and said, His
blood be on us and on our children.

Da gab er ihnen Barrabam los;
aber Jesum liess er geisseln, und über-
antwortete ihn, dass er gekreuziget
würde.

Then released he Barabbas unto
them: and when he had scourged Jesus, he delivered him to be crucified.

Recit.

Recit.

Erbarm es Gott!
Hier steht der Heiland angebunden.

[60] Have pity, God!
Here stands the Saviour bound and
    bleeding.

O Geisselung, o Schläg', o Wunden!

O stop the blows, the wounds, the
    scourging!

Ihr Henker haltet ein!
Erweichet euch
Der Seelenschmerz,
Der Anblick solches Jammers nicht?
Ach ja! ihr habt ein Herz,
Das muss der Martersäule gleich,
Und noch viel härter sein.
Erbarmt euch, haltet ein!

O hangmen, ye must stop!
Do ye not melt
In pain of soul,
At seeing all such wretchedness?
But no, ye must have hearts
Much like the scaffold is itself,
Or even harder still.
Have pity. Ye must stop!

Aria.

Aria.

Können Tränen meiner Wangen
Nichts erlangen,
  O! so nehmt mein Herz hinein.
Aber lasst es bei den Fluten,
Wenn die Wunden milde bluten
  Auch die Opferschale sein.
          Da Capo.

[61] If the teardrops on my cheeks
Naught avail,
  Then involve my heart as well.
But so let it in the flood,
When thy wounds are gently bleeding,
  Be the sacrificial cup.
          Da Capo.

The Mocking

Da nahmen die Kriegsknechte des
Landpflegers Jesum zu sich in das
Richthaus, und sammelten über ihn
die ganze Schar; und zogen ihn aus,
und legeten ihm einen Purpurmantel
an; und flochten eine Dornenkrone,
und setzten sie auf sein Haupt, und
ein Rohr in seine rechte Hand, und
beugeten die Knie vor ihm, und spott-
eten ihn, und sprachen: "Gegrüsset
seist du, Judenkönig!" Und speieten
ihn an, und nahmen das Rohr, und
schlugen damit sein Haupt.

[62] Then the soldiers of the governor
took Jesus into the common hall, and
gathered unto him the whole band of
soldiers. And they stripped him, and
put on him a scarlet robe. And when
they had platted a crown of thorns,
they put it upon his head, and a reed
in his right hand: and they bowed the
knee before him, and mocked him,
saying, Hail, King of the Jews! And
they spit upon him, and took the
reed, and smote him on the head.

Choral.

Chorale.

O Haupt, voll Blut und Wunden,
Voll Schmerz und voller Hohn!
O Haupt, zu Spott gebunden
Mit einer Dornenkron'!

[63] O head, now scourged and bleeding,
So full of pain and scorn!
O head, now mocked and circled
With such a crown of thorns!

O Haupt, sonst schön gezieret
Mit höchster Ehr' und Zier,
Jetzt aber hoch schimpfieret:
Gegrüsset seist du mir!

Du edles Angesichte,
Vor dem sonst schrickt und scheut
Das grosse Weltgewichte,
Wie bist du so bespeit!
Wie bist du so erbleichet,
Wer hat dein Augenlicht,
Dem sonst kein Licht nicht gleichet,
So schändlich zugericht'?

Und da sie ihn verspottet hatten, [64]
zogen sie ihm den Mantel aus, und
zogen ihm seine Kleider an und führeten ihn hin, dass sie ihn kreuzigten.
Und indem sie hinausgingen, fanden
sie einen Menschen von Kyrene, mit
Namen Simon; den zwangen sie, dass
er ihm sein Kreuz trug.

Recit.

Ja! freilich will in uns das Fleisch [65]
     und Blut
Zum Kreuz gezwungen sein;
Je mehr es unsrer Seele gut,
Je herber geht es ein.

Aria.

Komm, süsses Kreuz, so will ich [66]
     sagen,
   Mein Jesu, gib es immer her!
   Wird mir mein Leiden einst zu schwer,
So hilf du mir es selber tragen.
                        Da Capo.

Und da sie an die Stätte kamen, [67]
mit Namen Golgatha, das ist ver-
deutschet, Schädelstätt', gaben sie
ihm Essig zu trinken mit Gallen ver-
mischet; und da er's schmeckete,
wollte er's nicht trinken. Da sie ihn
aber gekreuziget hatten, teilten sie
seine Kleider, und wurfen das Los
darum; auf dass erfüllet würde, das
gesagt ist 'durch den Propheten: Sie

O head, adorned in beauty,
With honor once esteemed,
Now so grossly insulted:
Let me salute thee here!

Thou countenance so noble,
From whom once shrank in fear
The world's loftiest masters,
How art thou spat upon.
How pale thou art now growing,
Who hath thine eyes' fair light,
A light unlike all others,
So shamefully put out?

And after that they had mocked
him, they took the robe off from him,
and put his own raiment on him, and
led him away to crucify him. And as
they came out, they found a man of
Cyrene, Simon by name: him they
compelled to bear his cross.

Recit.

Yea, surely will the flesh and blood
     in us
Upon the cross be quelled:
The more for our souls' good,
The bitt'rer it will be.

Aria.

Come, sweet cross, I would be
     saying,
   My Jesu, always give it me.
   And if my suffering is too hard,
Then help me by myself to bear it.
                        Da Capo.

The Crucifixion

And, when they were come unto a
place called Golgotha, that is to say,
a place of a skull, they gave him vinegar to drink mingled with gall: and
when he had tasted thereof, he would
not drink. And they crucified him,
and parted his garments, casting lots:
that it might be fulfilled which was
spoken by the prophet, They parted
my garments among them, and upon

haben meine Kleider unter sich geteil-
et, und über mein Gewand haben sie
das Los geworfen. Und sie sassen alle
da, und hüteten sein. Und oben zu
seinem Haupte hefteten sie die Ursach' seines Todes beschrieben, näm-
lich: DIES IST JESUS, DER
JUDEN KOENIG. Und da wurden
zween Mörder mit ihm gekreuziget,
einer zur Rechten, und einer zur
Linken.

Die aber vorübergingen lästerten
ihn, und schüttelten ihre Köpfe, und
sprachen: "Der du den Tempel Gottes
zerbrichst, und bauest ihn in dreien
Tagen, hilf dir selber. Bist du Gottes
Sohn, so steig' herab vom Kreuz."
Desgleichen auch die Hohnenpriester
spotteten sein, samt den Schriftgelehrten und Altesten, und sprachen:
"Andern hat er geholfen, und kann
sich selber nicht helfen. Ist er der
König Israels, so steige er nun vom
Kreuz, so wollen wir ihm glauben. Er
hat Gott vertrauet, der erlöse ihn
nun, lüstet's ihn; denn er hat gesagt:
"Ich bin Gottes Sohn." Desgleichen [68]
schmäheten ihn auch die Mörder, die
mit ihm gekreuziget wurden.

my vesture did they cast lots. And sitting down they watched him there;
and set up over his head his accusations written, THIS IS JESUS THE
KING OF THE JEWS. Then were
there two thieves crucified with him,
one on the right hand, and another
on the left.

And they that passed by reviled
him, wagging their heads, and saying, Thou that destroyest the temple,
and buildest it in three days, save thyself. If thou be the Son of God, come
down from the cross. Likewise also
the chief priests mocking him, with
the scribes and elders, said, He saved
others; himself he cannot save. If he
be the King of Israel, let him now
come down from the cross; and we
will believe him. He trusted in God;
let him deliver him now, if he will
have him: for he said, I am the Son
of God.

The thieves also, which were crucified with him, cast the same in his
teeth.

Recit.
Zion.

Recit.
Zion.

Ach, Golgatha, unsel'ges Golgatha! [69]
Der Herr der Herrlichkeit muss
    schimpflich hier verderben,
Der Segen und das Heil der Welt
Wird als ein Fluch ans Kreuz gestellt.
Der Schöpfer Himmels und der Erden,
Soll Erd' und Luft entzogen werden;
Die Unschuld muss hier schuldig sterben.
Das gehet meiner Seele nah,
Ach, Golgatha, unsel'ges Golgatha!

Ah, Golgotha! accursed Golgotha!
The Lord of righteousness must
    come to grief insulted;
The Grace and blessing of the world
Will to the cross a curse be nailed.
The maker of the earth and heaven
Will have that earth and air denied.
The guiltless here is guilty dying,
It moves me to my very soul,
Ah, Golgotha! accursed Golgotha!

Aria à Duetto.
Zion und die Gläubigen.

Aria à Duetto.
Zion and the Faithful.

Z. Sehet, Jesus hat die Hand, [70]
Uns zu fassen ausgespannt,
Kommt! G. wohin? Z. In Jesus
    Armen,
Sucht Erlösung, nehmt Erbarmen.

Z. Look ye, Jesus hath his hand
Reaching out to clasp us fast.
Come F. Come where? Z. In Jesus'
    bosom
Seek redemption, take forgiveness.

Suchet. **G.** *wo?* **Z.** *in Jesus Armen.*
Lebet, sterbet, ruhet hier,
Ihr verlass'nen Küchlein ihr.
Bleibet! **G.** *wo?* **Z.** *in Jesus Armen.*

Seek ye! **F.** where? **Z.** in Jesus' bosom.
Live there, die there, rest ye there,
Ye forsaken little flock.
Stay there! **F.** where? **Z.** in Jesus' bosom.

The Final Agony

Und von der sechsten Stunde an [71]
ward eine Finsternis über das ganze
Land bis zu der neunten Stunde.
Und um die neunte Stunde schriee Je-
sus laut, und sprach: "Eli, Eli, lama,
lama, asabthani!" Das ist: "Mein
Gott, mein Gott, warum hast du
mich verlassen?" Etliche aber, die da
stunden, da sie das höreten, sprachen
sie: "Der rufet den Elias." Und bald
lief einer unter ihnen, nahm einen
Schwamm, und füllete ihn mit Essig,
und steckete ihn auf ein Rohr, und
tränkete ihn. Die andern aber sprach-
en: "Halt! Lass sehen, ob Elias
komme und ihm helfe." Aber Jesus
schriee abermal laut, und verschied.

Now from the sixth hour there was
darkness over all the land unto the
ninth hour. And about the ninth
hour Jesus cried with a loud voice,
saying, Eli, Eli, lama sabachthani?
that is to say, My God, my God, why
hast thou forsaken me? Some of them
that stood there, when they heard
that, said, This man calleth for Elias.
And straightway one of them ran, and
took a spunge, and filled it with vinegar, and put it on a reed, and gave
him to drink. The rest said, Let be,
let us see whether Elias will come to
save him. Jesus when he had cried
again with a loud voice, yielded up
the ghost.

Choral.

Chorale.

Wenn ich einmal soll scheiden, [72]
So scheide nicht von mir!
Wenn ich den Tod soll leiden,
So tritt du dann herfür!
Wenn mir am allerbängsten
Wird um das Herze sein,
So reiss' mich aus den Aengsten
Kraft deiner Angst und Pein!

When I at last must perish,
Do not depart from me!
And when I death must suffer,
So take me up to thee!
When to its final anguish
My heart is drawing near,
Then wrest me from that anguish
By virtue of thy pain!

Und siehe da, der Vorhang im [73]
Tempel zerriss in zwei Stück, von
oben an bis unten aus. Und die Erde
erbebete, und die Felsen zerrissen,
und die Gräber täten sich auf, und
stunden auf viel Leiber der Heiligen,
die da schliefen: und gingen aus den
Gräbern nach seiner Auferstehung,
und kamen in die heilige Stadt, und
erschienen vielen. Aber der Haupt-
mann, und die bei ihm waren, und
bewahreten Jesum, da sie sahen das
Erdbeben, und was da geschah, er-
schraken sie sehr, und sprachen:
"Wahrlich, dieser ist Gottes Sohn
gewesen."

And, behold, the veil of the temple
was rent in twain from the top to the
bottom; and the earth did quake, and
the rocks rent; and the graves were
opened; and many bodies of the saints
which slept arose, and came out of
the graves after his resurrection, and
went into the holy city, and appeared
unto many. Now when the centurion, and they that were with him,
watching Jesus, saw the earthquake,
and those things that were done, they
feared greatly, saying, Truly this was
the Son of God.

Und es waren viel Weiber da, die von Ferne zusahen, die da waren nachgefolget aus Galiläa, und hatten ihm gebienet: unter welchen war Maria Magdalena, und Maria, die Mutter Jacobi und Joses, und die Mutter der Kinder Zebedäi.

And many women were there beholding afar off, which followed Jesus from Galilee, ministering unto him: among which was Mary Magdalene, and Mary the mother of James and Joses, and the mother of Zebedee's children.

The Burial

Am Abend aber kam ein reicher Mann von Arimathia, der hiess Joseph, welcher auch ein Jünger Jesu war. Der ging zu Pilato, und bat ihn um den Leichnam Jesu. Da befahl Pilatus, man sollte ihm ihn geben.

When the even was come, there came a rich man of Arimathaea, named Joseph, who also himself was Jesus' disciple: he went to Pilate, and begged the body of Jesus. Then Pilate commanded the body to be delivered.

Recit.

Recit.

Am Abend da es kühle war, [74]
War Adams Fallen offenbar.
Am Abend drücket ihn der Heiland
    nieder;
Am Abend kam die Taube wieder,
Und trug ein Oelblatt in dem Munde.
O schöne Zeit! o Abendstunde!
Der Friedensschluss ist nun mit Gott
    gemacht,
Denn Jesus hat sein Kreuz vollbracht.
Sein Leichnam kommt zur Ruh.
Ach, liebe Seele, bitte du.
Geh, lasse dir den toten Jesum
    schenken,
O heilsames, o köstlich's
    Angedenken.

At evening, when the air was cool,
Was Adam's fall made manifest.
At evening too the Saviour was
    bow'd down;
At evening came the dove again,
And homeward bore an olive leaf.
O lovely time! O evening hour!
The peaceful end hath now been
    made with God,
For Jesus hath fulfilled his cross.
His body comes to rest.
Ah, dearest soul, I would pray,
Go, let dead Jesus thus for thee be
    offered,
A healing gift, so priceless a
    remembrance.

Aria.

Aria.

Mache dich, mein Herze, rein, [75]
Ich will Jesum selbst begraben,
    Denn er soll nunmehr in mir,
    Für und für,
Seine süsse Ruhe haben.
    Welt, geh aus, lass Jesum ein!
        Da Capo.

Make thee clean, my heart, from sin,
For there Jesus I would bury,
    That he may henceforth in me,
    More and more,
His most sweet repose be taking:
    World, depart, let Jesus in!
        Da Capo.

The Entombment

Und Joseph nahm den Leib, und [76]
wickelte ihn in ein rein' Leinwand.
Und legte ihn in sein eigen neu Grab,

And when Joseph had taken the body, he wrapped it in a clean linen cloth, and laid it in his own new

*welches er hatte lassen in einen Fels
hauen; und wälzete einen grossen
Stein vor die Tür des Grabes, und
ging davon. Es war aber allda Maria
Magdalena, und die andere Maria,
die satzten sich gegen das Grab.*

tomb, which he had hewn out in the
rock: and he rolled a great stone to the
door of the sepulchre, and departed.
And there was Mary Magdalene, and
the other Mary, sitting over against
the sepulchre.

The Securing of the Tomb

*Des andern Tages, der da folget
nach dem Rüsttage, kamen die
Hohenpriester und Pharisäer sämtlich
zu Pilato, und sprachen: "Herr, wir
haben gedacht, dass dieser Verführer
sprach, da er noch lebete: 'Ich will
nach dreien Tagen wieder auferstehen,' darum befiehl, dass man das
Grab verwahre bis an den dritten Tag,
auf dass nicht seine Jünger kommen,
und stehlen ihn, und sagen zu dem
Volk: 'Er ist auferstanden von den
Toten,' und werde der letzte Betrug
ärger, denn der erste." Pilatus sprach
zu ihnen: "Da habt ihr die Hüter:
gehet hin, und verwahret's, wie ihr
wisset." Sie gingen hin und verwahre-
ten das Grab mit Hütern, und versie-
gelten den Stein.*

Now the next day, that followed
the day of the preparation, the chief
priests and Pharisees came together
unto Pilate, saying, Sir, we remember that that deceiver said, while he
was yet alive, After three days I will
rise again. Command therefore that
the sepulchre be made sure until the
third day, lest his disciples come by
night, and steal him away, and say
unto the people, He is risen from the
dead: so the last error shall be worse
than the first. Pilate said unto them,
Ye have a watch: go your way, make
it as sure as ye can. So they went, and
made the sepulchre sure, sealing the
stone, and setting a watch.

Zion und die Gläubigen.

Z. *Nun ist der Herr zur Ruh
   gebracht,*
   G. *Mein Jesu, gute Nacht.*
Z. *Die Müh ist aus,
   Die unsre Sünden ihm gemacht,*

   G. *Mein Jesu, gute Nacht.*
Z. *O selige Gebeine!
   Seht, wie ich euch mit Buss und
      Reu beweine,
   Dass euch mein Fall in solche
      Not gebracht.*
   G. *Mein Jesu, gute Nacht!*
Z. *Habt lebenslang
   Vor euer Leiden tausend Dank,
   Dass ihr mein Seelenheil so wert
      geacht't.*
   G. *Mein Jesu, gute Nacht!*

Zion and the Faithful.

[77] **Z.** Now hath the Lord been laid to
   rest,
   F. My Jesus bid good night!
Z. Fatigue is gone,
   Which for our sins he long had
      borne,
   F. My Jesus bid good night!
Z. O holy limbs, most blessed,
   See how remorsefully I do repent
      me,
   That through my fall to such
      need thou wast brought.
   F. My Jesus bid good night!
Z. To thee, while life
   Shall last, I give a thousand thanks,
   That thou didst count my soul's
      salvation dear.
   F. My Jesus bid good night!

Aria Tutti.
Chor.

Aria Tutti.
Chorus.

Wir setzen uns mit Tränen nieder,   [78]
  Und rufen dir im Grabe zu:
  Ruhe sanfte! sanfte ruh!
Ruh't ihr ausgesognen Glieder!
  Euer Grab und Leichenstein
  Soll dem ängstlichen Gewissen
  Ein bequemes Ruhekissen
  Und der Seelen Ruhstatt sein.
Höchst vergnügt schlummern da die
  Augen ein.

Da Capo.

Here we sit down in tears and weeping,
  And call to thee now in the grave:
  Rest thou gently, gently rest!
Rest, exhausted, broken body!
  May thy tomb-stone and thy grave
  Be for our sore-troubled conscience
  A most comfortable cushion,
  And our souls' firm resting place.
High-esteem'd, close thine eyes and
  rest in sleep.

JOHANN SEBASTIAN BACH
An Interpretation of the Matthean Passion

The *Passion According to the Gospel of St. Matthew* was composed for use in the *Thomaskirche* in Leipzig during the Good Friday vesper service in the year 1729.[1] That purpose established a certain kinship between the Evangelist and the composer. Both Matthew and Bach had in mind an audience of Christian believers. The work of both men was used by a congregation engaged in worship, a worship centered in remembering the death and resurrection of Jesus and, to use the words of the eucharist in proclaiming "the Lord's death until he comes" (1 Cor. 11:26). Both the Gospel and the music were designed to stimulate intense reflection on the continuing implications of those events for the worshipers. Just as Matthew (we will use the traditional name for the author of this anonymous document) told the story in such a way as to bridge the distance in space and time between those earlier events and his own audience, so, too, Bach composed his music in such a way as to bridge the even greater distance to an eighteenth-century German congregation.[2]

We must not overlook the fact that both Bach and Matthew were engaged in telling a story, basically the same story. The cantor adopted the Matthean Passion story as a whole, without making a single change in the text as it came to him in Martin Luther's translation. Like the cantor, the Evangelist presented the story as a whole, the Passion being the longest single literary unit in his Gospel (chs. 26, 27). Both storytellers took care that their intended audiences would not react in a fragmentary way to a single isolated episode but in a unified way to the entire drama. Both believed that the events of the past anticipated and illuminated the story being lived by a Christian congregation in the present. For neither congregation was the story new, yet in each retelling new implications and

The quotations from the libretto come from four sources: Thomas Dunn's translation, my own translation, the RSV, and the Vox Stereo Recording (Album PL 6070).

reverberations emerged. Neither congregation was inclined to reduce the story to the bare bones of what had actually happened in Jerusalem or to the carefully formulated articles of a later creed. Each was invited to walk again down the cobblestones of the *Via Dolorosa*. In this study of Bach, therefore, one must recognize as of first importance this vital kinship between Evangelist and cantor and an equally vital kinship between their two audiences.

Visualizing Christian churches today may help us become aware of that kinship. The central symbol is usually a crucifix or a cross, a symbol that reminds worshipers of the story of a very specific crucifixion in all its gory and glorious details. It is that story that both Matthew and Bach recount in such a way as to set the life of the congregation within its orbit. To extend the analogy, in many sanctuaries the sacred space is marked off by the stations of the cross, suggesting that the life-journey of Christians, as well as of the Christ, proceeds from one station to the next. Both the Evangelist and the cantor provide guidance for those who walk along that road. In a recent essay depicting the relationship between Bach and Frederick the Great, O. L. Bettman makes the point that the emperor wrote music "to play by"; Bach wrote music "to pray by."[3]

In the structure of the *St. Matthew Passion* story the unifying strand is simply the narrative of Matthew, moving from the announcement of the coming crucifixion (26:1–2) to the burial in a guarded tomb (27:66). When the biblical narrative recounts points of special interest to the composer, he comments on those points. At times it is a specific word or an image that triggers his musical imagination; at times it is the significance of the episode as a whole that he tries to articulate. In examining his musical musings over the Gospel text, I will distinguish four types of material: the musical expression given to the biblical narrative; the chorales chosen by Bach himself from the hymnbook used by his congregation; the arias and recitatives in which Bach used poetic librettos written by Picander (the pseudonym of C. F. Henrici); and the dialogues between the "daughter of Zion" and "the Faithful," which are strategically placed.

The Narrative

The narrative takes the form of a succession of episodes, each increasing the dramatic tension. Attention shifts rapidly from one to another in a large cast of actors: Jesus, the disciples (with the spotlight turned on Peter and Judas), the crowds, the antagonists among the Jewish leaders, the Roman governor and his entourage. In Matthew each of these actors has a different role; Bach skillfully adapts the musical mood and intonation to express those roles.

When the Gospel is read, whether silently or orally, readers seldom pause to distinguish the various voices in the story. Part of Bach's contribution is a careful distinction among the dramatis personae. As one example, the Evangelist himself becomes a persona, playing a distinct role in the unfolding action, his tenor voice easily recognizable. Those who only read the Gospel silently often remain quite unconscious of the presence of this narrator, but those who hear the *Passion* discern his part clearly. To be sure, the voice of the narrator remains as unadorned, as impassive, almost as plain and impersonal, as the narrative itself (e.g., "the chief priests . . . gathered in the palace of the high priest" (Matt. 26:3). Yet just as Matthew's original audience recognized the narrator as one of their own leaders, probably a teacher,[4] so Bach helped his audience listen to the narrator as a person, a Christian believer who was speaking to them through the tenor soloist. And the steadily paced forward movement of the narrative, in itself quite colorless and laconic, adds realism to the increasing momentum and the sense of impending doom. The narrator is absorbed in the purposive thrust inherent in the story itself; and in the *St. Matthew Passion*, as Scheide insists, "the most purposive music combines with the most purposive book."[5] It is often a brief remark of the narrator (e.g., "he sought opportunity to betray him") that provokes the explosive protest of an aria or the poignant penitence of a chorale. The conversation thus activated between the audience and the Evangelist gives weight to the otherwise shadowy existence of that narrator. Surely, to create such a conversation is the essence of expert interpretation.

For Bach nothing in the Gospel text is more important than the voice of Jesus, which for him, as for Matthew, addresses later Christians as clearly as it did the earliest disciples. The baritone voice chosen for Jesus is distinct from the tenor of the Evangelist, covering a deeper range of resonances and colors. Whereas the prose of the narrator conveys austere, earthly objectivity, the words spoken by Jesus breathe an unearthly aura. They evoke a transcendent searching of minds and hearts, a probing insistence that demands some response. When Jesus announces, "one of you will betray me," his disciples respond with frenetic staccato questions, "Lord, is it I?" (cf. Mark 14:18–19; eleven times the word *Lord* is sung), and at once a chorale follows, giving the response of the Leipzig congregation, "It is I" [movement 15]. So the central dialogue throughout Matthew's Passion story consists of these responses elicited by Jesus' words. "The most tonally active regions of the *St. Matthew Passion* are centered around particular sayings of Jesus which Bach wished to emphasize."[6] Significantly, all these sayings relate in one way or another to the suffering of Jesus or of his disciples.

Moreover, Bach clearly understands Jesus' death, not as limited to the moments on the cross but as having taken place earlier. That death was actually present in Gethsemane when Jesus accepted the cross as God's will. It had been present even earlier when, at supper, he bestowed his flesh and blood as "priceless gifts." In fact, beginning with Jesus' baptism, Matthew pictured Jesus as having overcome the fear of death and as being concerned with helping his disciples to do the same (Matt. 4:1–11; 10:16–39).

Many musicologists have commented on the halo in sound that is placed around the head of Jesus by the strings' accompaniment of his words.[7] Significant when present, this halo is also significant when absent, as in the words of dereliction on the cross and in Jesus' refusal to give an answer to Pilate. So magisterial is the figure of Jesus in the Gospel story that one is confident that the words of Jesus that were spoken in the weeks before Golgotha would have been heard by Matthew's readers as the voice of their risen Lord. The same was true of Bach's audience. Those listeners were neither invited nor encouraged to identify themselves with Jesus, but they were called to respond to his words and deeds as a mysterious revelation of his Father's will. The figure of Jesus is as central in the *St. Matthew Passion* as in the Gospel.

Though Bach's listeners were not persuaded to identify themselves with Jesus, their identification with his disciples was constant, from the first aria to the last chorale.[8] One instance—the aria that is occasioned by the story of anointing—seems an exception, for the woman's devotion is contrasted to that of the original disciples, all of whom were male. Yet she also is a devout follower and thus fits a wider definition of *disciple*. In other passages Bach generally assumed that the term *disciples* represents all believers, male and female. Some reflections are more individual in tone, for example, the reply to Peter's pledge of loyalty: "I would stay here beside thee; O cast me not away"; but such individualism is a requirement of the scene. The fact that this "I" is sung as a chorale by the choir, representing the congregation, gives it a communal force. Other texts in Matthew, such as the saying "Let this cup pass from me" evoke a more inclusive reaction. Because the sins of the whole world have been poured into the cup, they exude a hateful stench. So in drinking the cup,

> The Savior falls down before his Father
> And thus lifts me *and all others*
> From our fall
> Back up to God's grace. [movement 28]

It is probable that Lutheran piety, the sieve through which Bach filtered the story, made the *St. Matthew Passion* more individualistic than the Gospel itself, for the first-person singular pronoun appears very frequently. However, Bach was intent also upon making a strong corporate confession.[9] To Pilate's query "what evil has he done?" the reply comes, "He has done good things *for us all*" [movement 57]. Later, I will elaborate this interest in the church when I discuss the opening and closing dialogues between the daughter of Zion and the Faithful. Here I simply wish to stress the strong accent on the role of Jesus' first disciples as precursors of later believers and on the character of the Gospel itself as a book that is devoted to their training. That same accent is surely part of Matthew's original intention.

The narrative assigns important roles to still other actors: Jewish rulers, false witnesses, Barabbas, the Roman judge and his soldiers. Neither Matthew nor Bach encourages listeners to identify themselves with any of these. No other individual attracts Bach as Peter and Judas do. He does not treat the religious and political opponents of Jesus as enemies of his audience, nor does he spend much time instructing Christians on how they should treat such opponents. He does not indulge in anti-Jewish or anti-Roman polemic. With regard to Pilate he is content to use a pun to call attention to the contrast between the earthly governor (*Landpflege*) [movement 56] and God, the always faithful governor (*Pflege*) [movement 53] of the heavens. To convey an idea of how Christians should view the whole array of Jesus' enemies, both religious and political, Bach uses a chorale prayer, "from all false malice shield me." He also prohibits vengeance: "in persecution be silent." Bach, of course, faced a very different situation from that of the Evangelist. Matthew's audience was undergoing violent persecution from successors of the enemies of Jesus. Because Bach's audience had few enemies of that sort, the early Christian warfare had lost much of its relevance. Yet both authors were agreed on excluding malice, hatred, violence. To both, Jesus' example and teaching excluded any recourse to vengeance against perpetrators of injustice, as well as any despair over the manifest power of evil.

The Chorales

The fifteen chorale verses (five of which come from a single chorale, *O Sacred Head Now Wounded*) are clues to Bach's understanding of the Passion story. Competent historical scholars attribute the selection of these verses to the composer.[10] Did the congregation in the *Thomaskirche* join in singing these chorales during the Good Friday performance of the *St. Matthew Passion*? Most scholars doubt it. Clearly Bach composed fresh harmonizations for each of the chorales. But it is also clear that the chorale texts were well known to the congregation, and knowledge of the words would have increased their sense of active participation not only in the music but in the events celebrated by the music.

Several observations may be safely made about the chorale texts as a whole. They are saturated with references to the death of Jesus, a natural focus of attention on Good Friday. The chorales place the whole story of crucifixion within the frame of a worldview in which God is indeed God. It is he who assigns a course to every cloud and every wind, controlling the whole sweep of history as well as each daily circumstance. Whatever God wills is what actually happens. This strategic assurance is located as a direct sequel to the prayer in Gethsemane; thus Jesus' own petition is echoed in the response of the congregation:

> . . . Whoever trusts God,
> builds firmly on him,
> will never be forsaken. [movement 31]

In the same way, everything depends on the goodness of God's rule over all things. This is true even when people choose evil. As everyone knows, when Peter heard the cock crow "he went out and wept bitterly" (Matt. 26:75). To that statement, Bach assigns this reaction to the congregation: "If from you I oft have fallen, I place myself back with you again." And there follows a firm assurance, "Your mercy and grace far outweigh the sins" [movement 48].

Every interpreter of the Passion must deal with Jesus' silence under the interrogation by Pilate. Jesus "gave him no answer . . . so that the governor wondered greatly" (Matt. 27:14). What meaning did that silence convey? Bach has an answer. He implies, by selecting the chorale verse that immediately follows, that Jesus' silence expressed a total freedom from fear and that this freedom came from a total reliance upon God. The story called Christians to show similar reliance:

> Commit your path
> And whatever sickens your heart
> To the all-faithful governor . . . .[movement 53]

Because Jesus lived and died to God, his death summons disciples to do the same. The music is God-obsessed, as is the Gospel.[11]

It is not strange that chorales chosen by a teacher of the Lutheran catechism should be saturated with the Lutheran spirit and the Pauline idiom. Bach chose hymns that give voice to the subtle associations between the death of Jesus and sin. Because Jesus was wholly guiltless, his death was to sin, for sin, for others, and for all humankind. These same chorales express the linkage between sin and the law, for Golgotha is seen as an accursed place, where "the grace and salvation of the world will be nailed as a curse to the cross" [movement 69]. Furthermore, Jesus' struggle with death represents a struggle with all the cosmic powers, including Satan. Those powers acted in fear of Jesus; in contrast, he won a victory over them by his fearlessness. In both the *St. Matthew Passion* and the Gospel this struggle became most intense in Gethsemane when Jesus became "sorrowful, even to death" (Matt. 26:38). Now the tortures of hell struck the hardest, and divine help seemed most distant [movements 24, 25]. This death before death is symbolized by Jesus' falling to the ground, an atoning and elevating action no less significant to Bach than the crucifixion itself.[12] Nor did Jesus' death begin only in Gethsemane; it had been anticipated in the Bethlehem massacre. In the words of the chorale "he was *born* to be the mediator for all mankind." So the chorales assign the work of atonement to the whole story, making it the source of life for Christians and therefore a pattern for them to obey.

Now a comment on the strategic location and thrust of the second chorale [movement 3]. It comes as soon as the tenor (the narrator) and the baritone (Jesus) have made the ominous disclosure that the Son of man will be crucified (Matt. 26:2). Because congregations, whether in Matthew's day, in Bach's day, or in ours, are familiar with the story and already know what follows, they usually allow this announcement to pass without any sense of surprise or consternation. Not so Bach. The son of man . . . crucified? The chorale interrupts the narrative with an immediate, violent revulsion. "Dearest Jesus, what crime have you committed that such a harsh sentence has been given?" Almost before it starts, the story is halted, and listeners are forced to take fresh notice of several facts: the innocence of Jesus, the affection in which he is held, the cruel injustice he must suffer. All this with an emotional vehemence that suggests nothing less than cosmic reverberations. Matthew is content with the restrained, austere announcement; Bach is content with nothing less than spontaneous horror. His congregation was familiar with the melody of the chorale, sung a capella. Bach harmonizes that melody to bring out more clearly his sense of intolerable contradiction. In his hands the chorale functions in ways similar to the hymns in the book of Revelation.

Some chorales are linked to the Scripture more by a single word than by the episode as a whole. An example is the response to Matthew 26:31–33, in which Jesus, in leading the disciples from the Upper Room to the Mount of Olives, makes several predictions, all very important to Matthew: all disciples will be caused to stumble, the shepherd will be struck down, the sheep will be scattered, and Jesus will precede them to Galilee after his resurrection. None of these predictions aroused the composer's musical imagination. Rather, he was attracted to the image of a shepherd and his flock; so he chose a hymn verse to articulate a Christian's dependence as a sheep on Christ as a good shepherd [movement 21]. This motif is implicit, of course, in the text, but it bears little direct relationship to the tense moment described by Matthew.

Arias and Recitatives

Because the librettos for these sections of the *St. Matthew Passion* were written by Picander, all the motifs cannot be assigned to Bach, even though the poet worked under his close supervision. Yet there are subtle contrasts between the chorales and the arias. The chorales are more expressive of group sentiments; the arias are more individual. The chorales are more traditional; the arias more innovative. In accepting Picander's poetry, however, Bach must have given it some degree of approval. The words are not Bach's, but the musical medium is his. Of that medium, Albert Schweitzer's observation is sound:

> Bach now and then heightens the sentiment of his text in the most striking way; he turns contentment into exultant joy, and grief into violent despair. . . . When he translates a feeling into tone, he voices it in its extreme form.[13]

As a result one senses an emotional vitality that is lacking in most academic interpretations. The composer conveyed in music a virtually unlimited range of feelings: from a low degree of lethargy to a high degree of energy, from hesitant indecision to explosive action, from seething anger to soothing tranquillity. Often particular instruments are chosen to suggest the affection that dominates a movement. Steinitz calls attention to the use of recorders to bring out the pathos in the words, the *oboé da caccia* to connote moments of anguish, flutes to represent the falling of tears, horns and timpani to accompany royalty, the slow, steady pulse of the basses to mark the steps on the road toward Golgotha.[14]

As in the chorales, so in the arias the dominant emotions are those that characterize the bond between the disciples and their Lord. So volatile, so spontaneous, are these emotions that it becomes quite impossible to think of the disciples as impersonal puppets acting out their prescribed parts on an ancient stage. They are fully alive, perhaps too much so. They are so vigorous and so insistent in their protestations that one is inclined to say that the composer "must have thought God a little hard of hearing."[15]

A good example is the alto aria that follows Matthew's account of the anointing of Jesus (26:6–13). The Scripture narrative is impassive and austere, but Bach and Picander join in articulating highly charged under-currents. They treat the ointment as the woman's tears (unmentioned in the Gospel), and the falling of the tears may be heard in "overlapping downward arpeggios."[16] The tears in turn express the anguish (again, un-mentioned in the Gospel) that arises from a heart sundered by sin: "Peni-tence tears in two the sinful heart" [movements 9, 10]. Because the sin is not identified, it can be taken as representing all sins and all sinners. The weeping becomes a form of sacrifice offered to Jesus in view of his ap-proaching death (as in the Gospel), an ointment to prepare his body for burial. As in the Gospel, the death of Jesus casts its shadow over every-thing that precedes it.

This colorful portrait of the woman shares the same frame as the sorry picture of the disciples, who in the name of the poor angrily opposed such waste. Their anger, marked by short, jagged phrases and by ugly chro-matic intervals, adds its own emphasis to the woman's grief.[17] The inci-dent portrays a sinner as righteous and the righteous as sinners, a disclosure that the approaching events could only confirm. Listeners are naturally inclined to think of themselves in the role of the woman:

> Penitence
>   Tears my sinning heart in two,
> Let the teardrops of my weeping
>   Soothing spices ever be,
>   Beloved Jesu, offered thee.[18]

Again, the disciples receive rough treatment, this time in the aria that follows Judas' bargain with the priests to betray Jesus (Matt. 26:14–15). A soprano dramatizes the agony that Jesus felt at this act of treason, as well as the soloist's own grief for Jesus [movement 12]. The infant nourished at the breast has become a poisonous snake. Grief is suggested by the de-scending line of the flutes; the snake's presence is suggested by the sinuous curling of the *básso contínuo*.[19] So interpreted, the words link Judas' be-trayal to the primeval sin in the Garden (Gen. 3:1) and thereby link Jesus' grief over Judas to his grief over the cumulative sin of the race, thus tying his victory to victory over that legacy. Several deaths are seen to be present in this one death: the deaths of Adam and Eve, of Judas, of Jesus, and all deaths due to the sin that is rightly called original.

A different range of emotions is released by the account of the Last Supper (26:26–29): first by the narrative itself [movement 17], then by a recitative [movement 18], and finally by an aria [movement 19]. The mu-sic of the narrative itself pictures Jesus' inner serenity and quiet confidence in the future, with no suggestion of grief or fear. He speaks, as if in the past tense, of his blood of the new testament; he gives a final bequest to his disciples; and he pledges to eat with them in his Father's kingdom.[20] In response, the recitative articulates several of the basic emotions imbedded in the eucharist, especially in Good Friday devotions:

> Although my heart swims in tears, because Jesus must depart, still his testament makes me rejoice. His flesh and blood, O priceless gift, he bequeaths to me. When he was in the world among his own, he intended no evil. He loved them to the end. [movement 18]

The death of Jesus fuses sorrow and joy, proving the enduring power of his love (Picander here draws a line from John 13:1). It conveys a bequest of his flesh and blood, which are given "to me" as bread and wine. Such affections are indigenous to the sacrament as anticipations of the supper in the Father's kingdom.

The aria that follows moves even further toward expressing the depth of eucharistic devotion:

> I would offer my heart to you. Pervade me, my salvation. I would lose myself in you. As the world seems too small to you, so to me you alone shall be more than earth and heaven. [movement 19]

The Savior enters the heart of the worshiper, who is lost in the Savior. So overwhelming is this transformation in perspectives that the world becomes small to Jesus, and to worshipers, Jesus becomes larger than the world. The Bach interpreter can speak here, with some justification, of a mystical union, though a better term might well be a musical union, between Christ and his church.

A quite different mood pervades the recitative that accompanies the scourging (Matt. 27:26) [movement 60]. Here the torture of the convicted criminal provokes a loud outcry. The singer appeals to God to have pity and shouts out a demand to the soldiers, "Hangman, stop! Stop the blows! Stop the wounds!" But the hearts of the soldiers prove even harder than the wood of the scaffold. Yet the music does not indicate so much a hatred of those men as the culpability of all Christians.

Characteristic of many recitatives is the answer to Pilate's question "what evil has he done?" (Matt. 27:23). In the Gospel that question was addressed to the Jewish antagonists. Bach, with Picander's assistance, asks the question of followers and gives an answer that includes the Leipzig worshipers:

> He hath done good things for us all,
> A blind man he gave back his sight,
> A lame man made he walk,
> He told us of his Father's Word,

He drove the devil out,
Those troubled hath he comforted,
He took upon himself our sins,
Naught else hath Jesus ever done.[21] [movement 57]

That answer stands as the epitome of the mission of Jesus; its accuracy as a summary of Matthew can hardly be challenged.

Six Dialogues

On six strategic occasions, the *St. Matthew Passion* features conversations between two characters, the daughter of Zion and the Faithful. It was probably to give a separate identity to these two that Bach used two choruses. Each dialogue is initiated by the daughter of Zion, who usually invites the Faithful to reflect upon previous or coming events. Because neither of these characters appears in the Matthean Passion story, Picander was free to invent their words. In doing this, he was following a practice adopted by earlier composers, but their roles are anything but accidental or capricious. Each dialogue appears at a highly strategic moment, and each is designed to give listeners something of a panoramic view of what is happening. They give a wider historical frame for the story. The key to their roles is the biblical image of the daughter of Zion, who appears in the Matthean narrative when Jesus arrives in Jerusalem to celebrate the Passover.

This took place to fulfill what was spoken by the prophet: "Tell the daugher of Zion, see, your king is coming to you, humble, and mounted on an ass, and on a colt, the foal of an ass." (Matt. 21:4–5, author's translation)

So we recognize in the daughter of Zion the one to whom God has promised a king. She is the people to whom this king comes, the one addressed first by the prophets. To her, Isaiah had called, "See, your salvation comes" (62:11, author's translation). She is the one whom Zechariah urged, "Rejoice greatly" (9:9). She is the messianic community in whom and for whom the law and the prophets are fulfilled. Unlike the chief priests and the elders, who reject the Messiah's credentials (Matt. 21:23–43), she accepts them. It is in representing this true Israel that the daughter of Zion initiates the conversations with the Faithful. Whom, then, did the Faithful represent in Bach's scenario? Like the daughter of Zion, she seems to represent a group, but a group somewhat distinct from that of the daughter of Zion. She may be intended to symbolize the Gentiles, who from the beginning of Jesus' work had been present as those Galileans who "sat in the region and shadow of death" and on whom the "light has dawned" (Matt. 4:16). Or the Faithful may represent more generally all believers, of whatever racial or economic origin. In any case, the two choruses represent larger communities who could not be represented on center stage but whose presence in the wings both Matthew and Bach recognized, the daughter of Zion speaking for the messianic mother and the Faithful for all believers in him. Other episodes and arias helped to modernize the story as if they were happening in Germany in 1729; these dialogues helped to archaize the Good Friday story, so that worshipers shared again in that ancient setting of sharp conflict between believing and unbelieving Jews, and between Gentile believers and Jews.

The first of these dialogues introduces the entire oratorio:

Daughter of Zion:	Come, daughters, join me in weeping. Look!
The Faithful:	At whom?
Daughter of Zion:	The Bridegroom. Look at him!
The Faithful:	How?
Daughter of Zion:	As a lamb! [movement 1]

Here the daughter of Zion chorus takes over the role accorded in Matthew to the prophecies of Isaiah and Zechariah. In addition, the daughter of Zion uses the two seemingly incongruous images, the bridegroom and the lamb, to call to mind the primary New Testament ways of referring to Jesus as Messiah. No images in Scripture have a richer resonance. The bride welcomes the advent of the bridegroom, but followers must learn to recognize him in the humiliation of a lamb. The following chorale makes this paradox the subject of successive ejaculations:

Daughter of Zion:	O, innocent lamb of God, Slaughtered on a cross. Look!
The Faithful:	At what?
Daughter of Zion:	Look at his patience, even when despised. Look!
The Faithful:	On what?
Daughter of Zion:	On our guilt. [movement 1]

The bride thus identifies the bridegroom (cf. Matt. 25: 1–13) by pointing to those very features that induced the rulers of Israel to despise him, lamblike innocence and patience. This highly charged interchange serves as a preview of all that is to follow, and the daughter of Zion's call to the Faithful is a call addressed to the worshipers in Leipzig.

The character of the music supports this analysis. Bach pictures the noisy crowds on the streets of Jerusalem, in turmoil over the news of the day, unsettled by messianic excitements. The distraught music imparts a sense of tension, of rough jostling, of restless anticipation. Bach "saw Jesus being led through the town to the cross; his eye caught sight of the crowd surging through the streets; he heard them calling and answering each other."[22] In the midst of this confusion, the daughter of Zion invites the Faithful to hail the bridegroom in the shameful figure of the slain lamb. Such an introduction gives an epic sweep to each successive scene.

The second dialogue continues to orient numerous details within the same framework. One such detail is the sorrow of Jesus in Gethsemane, "even unto death," along with his futile appeal to his disciples to watch with him. As if from offstage, the omniscient daughter of Zion calls the attention of the Faithful to the torment, inducing the Faithful to ask the reason for such suffering [movement 25]. In reply the daughter of Zion summons up the background of God's final judgment: hell itself is implicated in Jesus' agony. This statement enables the Faithful to recognize that the true reason for the torment is human sinning. "I only am guilty of what you suffer." Then the two choruses—the daughter of Zion and the Faithful—join in a duet in which they define the watching: to keep awake with Jesus means that their sins fall asleep [movement 26]. They confess together that Jesus' suffering atones for "my death," conveying all the bitterness and sweetness of that awareness. Bach thus sees the Gethsemane story as the enactment of an ultimate judgment and an ultimate redemption, an example, in Pauline terms, of a death-to-sin that atones for a universal death-in-sin.

The third dialogue emerges in connection with Jesus' arrest: "They came . . . laid hands on Jesus . . . seized him" (Matt. 26:50). In a brief conversation the daughter of Zion calls the attention of the Faithful to what has happened: "So my Jesus has now been seized." Then two violent protests from the Faithful: "Stop! Don't tie him up!" but those protests are futile. Then the daughter of Zion interprets the disaster in cosmic terms: for shame at Judas' act, the moon hides its face. Together, the daughter of Zion and the Faithful sing of Judas' kiss as the opening of hell's abyss; they use language both verbal and musical to link this "murderous blood" to all the injustice and violence in history, since the days of Cain. This choral duet helps to mark the climax of the dramatic action in part 1 [movement 33].

The fourth dialogue introduces part 2, the music that followed the sermon on Good Friday. For the moment the stage is empty, and there is silence. Jesus has been seized, and his disciples have fled. Now the daughter of Zion and the Faithful point ahead to the coming trial and execution. The daughter of Zion asks, "Where has my Jesus gone?" and the Faithful echoes, "Where has your friend gone?" The daughter of Zion knows that her "lamb" is being held in "tiger's claws," and the Faithful announces her readiness to go with the daughter of Zion to seek Jesus [movement 36]. Then the narrative returns to the palace of the high priest.

The fifth dialogue, occasioned by the crucifixion, carries the thought a step further. Because only the enemies of Jesus are now onstage, the comments of the daughter of Zion and the Faithful appear to bespeak an offstage explanation of what is happening. In a long recitative the daughter of Zion tells how the Creator of heaven and earth has decided that the blessing and salvation of the world should be nailed to the cross as a curse, the guiltless dying for the guilty. Following this explanation comes an impassioned invitation:

Daughter of Zion: Come
The Faithful: Where?
Daughter of Zion: To Jesus' arms . . . Live there, die there, rest there, re-
                             main there, you forsaken little flock. [movement 70]

Each verb in this invitation is drawn from the New Testament vocabulary of salvation. The nearest verbal equivalent may be found in the invitation Matthew attributed to Jesus himself (11:25–30). Although the Evangelist locates this saying during the earthly ministry, many scholars believe that it probably originated in the postresurrection period as a prophetic word relayed from the risen Christ. Whichever time is accurate, both Matthew and Bach use the invitation to encapsulate the entire Gospel.

The composer places the sixth dialogue at the very end, after the guard has been posted at the tomb, when all others have departed. Now, as earlier, the daughter of Zion tells the Faithful what has happened, and the Faithful voices the reactions of the followers. The daughter of Zion assures the Faithful that Jesus is at last at rest and acknowledges the fall, which made that death necessary. The mood is one of penitence and gratitude. In response the Faithful repeats the simple farewell "My Jesus, good night" [movements 77, 78]. The music surrounds the congregation with an atmosphere of quiet gentleness and comforting tranquillity. The Good Friday service comes to an end with music adapted to meditation and benediction.

✳✳✳

In summary, Bach, in his treatment of Matthew's narrative, showed a very high respect for Scripture as a revelation of God's presence throughout the story of Jesus. In his reliance upon the chorales, he reflected loyalty to the Lutheran tradition and sensitivity to the church's liturgical customs. His use of the arias and recitatives manifests an imaginative richness in expressing a wide range of religious affections and an extreme intensity of individual feeling. The dialogues between the daughter of Zion and the Faithful broaden the perspectives within which to understand the death of Jesus: the history of Israel as a covenant community to which God has given the law and the prophets; the inclusive archetypal images of the sin of Adam and the murder of Abel; the cosmic work of the Creator, along with intuitions of his final judgment on all humankind. All this constitutes a genuine and impressive interpretation of Scripture.

After describing the magisterial musical accomplishments of this composer, Percy M. Young ventures his belief that Bach "held a point of view that in modern times is unintelligible."[23] I grant Mr. Young his right to that judgment, and in addition I grant that one can amass much evidence to support it. However, I must say that, coming to this music from the world of the Bible and from the idiom of Matthew, I find Bach's point of view wholly intelligible. Many listeners to the Passion would, I think, agree; they would not respond to utter nonsense as deeply as they continue to respond to this music. Whether or not we find Bach's faith acceptable is, of course, another matter. And before we can decide the question of acceptability, we need to ponder the distinctively biblical and Matthean perceptions of death—the many kinds and degrees of death, the death of sinners, the death of Jesus, along with the corresponding perceptions of life, especially the power of that life, which, according to both Matthew and Bach, was released through the Passion.[24]

JOHANNES BRAHMS

A German Requiem

A GERMAN REQUIEM

Johannes Brahms

Adapted from the German by E. M. Traquair; revised by R. H. Benson.
Reproduced by permission C. F. Peters Corporation, New York,
on behalf of the copyright owner, Peters Edition, Ltd., London.

I

Selig sind, die da Leid tragen,
denn sie sollen getröstet werden.
Die mit Tränen säen,
werden mit Freuden ernten.
Sie gehen hin und weinen
und tragen edlen Samen
und kommen mit Freuden
und bringen ihre Garben.

II

Denn alles Fleisch ist wie Gras
und alle Herrlichkeit des Menschen
wie des Grases Blumen.
Das Gras ist verdorret
und die Blume abgefallen.
So seid nun geduldig, lieben Brüder,
bis auf die Zukunft des Herrn.
Siehe, ein Ackermann wartet
auf die köstliche Frucht der Erde
und ist geduldig darüber,
bis er empfahe
den Morgenregen
und Abendregen.
Denn alles Fleisch ist wie Gras
und alle Herrlichkeit des Menschen
wie des Grases Blumen.
Das Gras ist verdorret
und die Blume abgefallen.
Aber des Herrn Wort
bleibet in Ewigkeit.
Die Erlöseten des Herrn
werden wieder kommen

I

Blessed are they that mourn, for
they shall have comfort.
They that sow in tears shall reap in
joy.
Who goeth forth and weepeth, and
beareth precious seed, shall doubtless
return with rejoicing, and bring his
sheaves with him.

II

Behold, all flesh is as the grass, and
all the goodliness of man is as the
flower of grass; for lo, the grass
with'reth, and the flower thereof
decayeth.
Now, therefore, be patient, O my
brethren, unto the coming of Christ.
See how the husbandman waiteth
for the precious fruit of the earth, and
hath long patience for it, until he receive the early rain and the latter
rain.
So be ye patient.
Albeit the Lord's word endureth for
evermore.
The redeemed of the Lord shall return again, and come rejoicing unto
Zion; gladness, joy everlasting, joy
upon their heads shall be; joy and
gladness, these shall be their portion,
and tears and sighing shall flee from
them.

und gen Zion kommen mit Jauchzen;
ewige Freude wird über ihrem Haupte sein,
Freude und Wonne werden sie ergreifen,
und Schmerz und Seufzen wird weg müssen.

III

Herr, lehre doch mich,
dass ein Ende mit mir haben muss,
und mein Leben ein Ziel hat,
und ich davon muss.   [*dir,*
Siehe, meine Tage sind einer Hand
*   breit vor*
und mein Leben ist wie nichts vor dir.
Ach, wie gar nichts sind alle
*   Menschen,*
die doch so sicher leben.
Sie gehen daher wie ein Schemen
und machen ihnen viel vergebliche Unruhe,
sie sammeln und wissen nicht,
wer es kriegen wird.
Nun, Herr, wes soll ich mich trösten?
Ich hoffe auf dich.
Der Gerechten Seelen sind in Gottes Hand,
und keine Qual rühret sie an.

IV

Wie lieblich sind deine Wohnungen,
Herr Zebaoth!
Meine Seele verlanget und sehnet sich
nach den Vorhöfen des Herrn;
mein Leib und Seele freuen sich
in dem lebendigen Gott.
Wohl denen, die in deinem Hause
wohnen,
die loben dich immerdar.

V

Ihr habt nun Traurigkeit,
aber ich will euch wieder sehen,
und euer Herz soll sich freuen,
und eure Freude soll niemand von euch
*   [nehmen.*
Sehet mich an:
Ich habe eine kleine Zeit
Mühe und Arbeit gehabt
und habe grossen Trost funden.
Ich will euch trösten,
wie einen seine Mutter tröstet.

III

Lord, make me to know the measure of my days on earth, to consider my frailty that I must perish.

Surely, all my days here are as an handbreadth to Thee, and my lifetime is as naught to Thee.

Verily, mankind walketh in a vain show, and their best state is vanity.

Man passeth away like a shadow, he is disquieted in vain, he heapeth up riches, and cannot tell who shall gather them.

Now, Lord, O, what do I wait for? My hope is in Thee.

But the righteous souls are in the hand of God, nor pain, nor grief shall nigh them come.

IV

How lovely is Thy dwelling place, O Lord of Hosts!

For my soul, it longeth, yea fainteth for the courts of the Lord; my soul and body crieth out, yea, for the living God.

O blest are they that dwell within Thy house; they praise Thy name evermore!

V

Ye now are sorrowful, howbeit ye shall again behold me, and your heart shall be joyful, and your joy no man taketh from you.

Yea, I will comfort you, as one whom his own mother comforteth.

Look upon me; ye know that for a little time labour and sorrow were mine, but at the last I have found comfort.

VI

Denn wir haben hie keine bleibende Statt,
sondern die zukünftige suchen wir.
Siehe, ich sage euch ein Geheimnis:
Wir werden nicht alle entschlafen,
wir werden aber alle verwandelt werden;
und dasselbige plötzlich, in einem
            [Augenblick,
zu der Zeit der letzten Posaune.
Denn es wird die Posaune schallen,
und die Toten werden auferstehen
unverweslich,
und wir werden verwandelt werden.
Dann wird erfüllet werden
das Wort, das geschrieben steht:
Der Tod ist verschlungen in den Sieg.
Tod, wo ist dein Stachel?
Hölle, wo ist dein Sieg?
Herr, du bist würdig zu nehmen
Preis und Ehre und Kraft,
denn du hast alle Dinge geschaffen,
und durch deinen Willen haben sie das
             [Wesen
und sind geschaffen.

VII

Selig sind die Toten, die in dem Herrn
            [sterben, von nun an.
Ja, der Geist spricht, dass sie ruhen von
            [ihrer Arbeit;
denn ihre Werke folgen ihnen nach.

VI

Here on earth have we no continuing place, howbeit, we seek one to
come.

Lo, I unfold unto you a mystery.

We shall not all sleep when He
cometh, but we shall all be changed
in a moment, in a twinkling of an
eye, at the sound of the trumpet.

For the trumpet shall sound, and
the dead shall be raised incorruptible,
and all we shall be changed.

Then, what of old was written, the
same shall be brought to pass.

For death shall be swallowed in
victory!

Death, O where is thy sting?

Grave, where is thy triumph?

Worthy art Thou to be praised,
Lord of honour and might, for thou
hast earth and heaven created, and
for Thy good pleasure all things have
their being, and were created.

VII

Blessed are the dead which die in
the Lord from henceforth.

Sayeth the spirit, that they rest
from their labours, and that their
works follow after them.

JOHANNES BRAHMS
A Requiem for Humankind

The year 1983 marked the 150th anniversary of the birth of Johannes Brahms, and the occasion was celebrated throughout the world by musicians in orchestral and choral groups. Perhaps never before have so many people heard the longest and, according to many critics, the greatest of his choral works, *A German Requiem*. In this study of the composition I will concentrate on Brahms' interpretation of the biblical citations. The objectives will be the same as those in the preceding chapter, though I will not try to establish any comparison between the two composers. Brahms included Bach among those musicians to whom he owed the greatest debt. When he referred to the two outstanding events of the nineteenth century, he mentioned, along with the founding of the German Empire, the publication of the complete edition of the works of Bach.[1]

Scholars have found themselves unable to agree on the appraisal of Brahms' religious loyalties and affections. It is true, of course, that this composer never held a musical post in the church and that he designed his music for the concert hall rather than the sanctuary, even though the *German Requiem* was first performed in the Bremen cathedral on April 10, 1868. But there is little doubt that Brahms had an extensive and discriminating knowledge of the Bible in the Luther translation.[2] His mother had taken seriously her responsibility for the moral and religious training of her three children. In primary school, also, the boy had listened to daily Bible readings. According to Karl Geiringer, Brahms "boasted that he could always instantly lay his hand on those books he valued—for example, the Bible—even in the dark."[3]

The quotations from the libretto are from the RSV, my own translation, or C. F. Peters Vocal Score (English text, No. 3672a).

The texts chosen for the *German Requiem* reveal much about his familiarity with the Bible and his best-loved passages. In selecting them he refused to follow either the tradition of the Catholic mass for the dead or any Protestant lectionary, insisting rather on choosing his own. The primary selections were apparently made during a day spent in the woods near Hamburg, where he was indulging his lifelong love of nature.[4] Citations were chosen from fifteen chapters of eleven books in the Old Testament, the New Testament, and the Apocrypha.[5] In several movements Brahms worked as a weaver, interlacing quotations from both Testaments. Citations from the New Testament received the stronger accent, and many of them provide the frame in which other texts are set. Unlike Bach, Brahms limited himself to the Bible, so his interpretation is conveyed by the sequence and arrangements of the citations. There is an overarching architectural plan, even though later reconstructions of the original blueprint fail to be wholly convincing.[6] The existence of such a plan is reflected in the strategic placement of three beatitudes. The work begins with a beatitude from Matthew and closes with one from the Apocalypse; in between, the central movement ends with a beatitude from Psalm 84. The following chart illustrates the range and diversity of the quotations.

Texts

Movement	Primary	Secondary
1	Matthew 5:4	Isaiah 61:2–3
	Psalm 126:5–6	
2	1 Peter 1:24	Isaiah 40:6,7
	James 5:7–8	Deuteronomy 11:14
		Joel 2:23
	1 Peter 1:25	Isaiah 40:8
	Isaiah 35:10	
3	Psalm 39:4–7	
	Wisdom of Solomon 3:1	
4	Psalm 84:1–2,4	
5	John 16:22	Isaiah 66:14
	Isaiah 66:13	
	Ecclesiasticus 51:27	Matthew 11:28
6	Hebrews 13:14	Revelation 21:2
	1 Corinthians 15:51–55	Isaiah 25:8
	Revelation 4:11	Hosea 13:14
7	Revelation 14:13	

It is impossible to recover a conscious motivation behind the selection of these texts and the rejection of others. Although Brahms obviously used great care in the selection, his criteria must always remain hidden. Some conjectures, however, are more convincing than others. For example, by starting with the beatitude from the Sermon on the Mount, he chose to introduce the work as a whole with a theme that applies to every movement. Moreover, the choice of this theme distinguishes his work from the traditional mass for the dead by shifting attention from the dead to the living, for whom the central problem is not the loss of loved ones or the moment of death but the many forms of mortality encountered throughout life.

Again, it is likely that he chose texts that were relatively free of confessional or sectarian slant. He thought of the work as "a human requiem," "addressed to all, irrespective of creed." He wanted to reach "the total community of mankind,"[7] whose experience of transience excludes parochial partisanship. This, for example, was the reason for excluding John 3:16.[8]

The biblical citations have some common features that may have attracted the eye of the composer. For example, they abound in poetic forms filled with images that invite musical expression. They reflect the perspectives of poets, psalmists, and prophets, whose vocation included the double task of voicing both God's speech to human beings (e.g., God is the assumed speaker in the beatitudes) and human responses to God (e.g., "Lord, let me know my end").[9] These seers were expert in transmuting all serious thinking about human existence into a dialogue with the Divine, whether in prayer or in protest. They had an eye for the invisible connections linking ordinary chores, such as the planting of grain, to the beginning and the end of all things. They assumed that whatever the immediate situation of an audience, it could consider itself the recipient of ancient revelations and could anticipate the fulfillment of promises made to long-dead generations. Such statements are supported only by the character of the texts. Whether or not the circumstantial evidence supports them can be evaluated by looking at the movements of the *German Requiem.*

Movement 1

a   "Blessed are those who mourn,
b   for they shall be comforted." (Matt. 5:4; also Isa. 61:2–3)
a   May those who sow in tears
b   reap with shouts of joy!
a   He that goes forth weeping, bearing the seed for sowing,
b   shall come home with shouts of joy, bringing his sheaves with him.
     (Ps. 126:5–6)

The Gospel sees in these words of Jesus the fulfillment of the promise that God had given to Israel. Both Isaiah and Matthew treat mourning as a figure that includes far more than mourning at the decease of a friend or a relative. By the same token, comfort includes much more than a word of solace offered to the bereaved.

That inclusiveness becomes clearer in a careful study of the antithetical parallelism embodied in the psalm, in which the lines marked *a* describe an action opposite that in the lines marked *b*. Sowing, in line *a*, is set against the reaping in line *b*; similarly, the weeping is set against the shouts of joy, and the going forth against the homecoming. Basic to these oppositions is a synonymous element: the three actions mentioned in lines *a* are viewed as equivalents—sowing, weeping, going forth. Each of these images qualifies the meaning of the other two. The three acts in line *b* are also viewed as equivalents—reaping, shouts of joy, homecoming— and, again, each image qualifies the others.

Now what happens when Brahms combines this psalm with the beatitude from Matthew? A fourth set of equivalents emerges from lines *a* and *b* of the Gospel. The meaning of mourning is qualified by the acts of sowing, weeping, and going forth. By the same logic, comfort expresses the same reality as reaping, shouts of joy, and homecoming. Four sets of contrasting but related activities give to each activity a breadth and depth that it would not otherwise have. But it is the conjunction of Gospel and psalm that alone makes this possible. Brahms was alone in seeing this conjunction, for no verbal link between the two documents calls attention to the kinship of thought. He alone discerned the correlation of pictures, and, significantly, this correlation appears in the first movement. From its beginning the *German Requiem* deals not only with grief at another's demise but with human mortality, including all forms of "going forth," all modes of "bearing seed for sowing," and all occasions that evoke tears. It is indeed a human requiem because of the range of experience conjured up by these cognate images.[10]

Such an introduction to a requiem is quite unexpected, whether one consults church or musical traditions; yet it is entirely indigenous to the biblical lexicon of images and to the poetic thought-forms characteristic of prophets and psalmists. Those ancient thinkers used the pictures of planting and harvesting, of exile and return, to conjure up the vast dimensions of human history. These are the forms that Brahms found eminently capable of musical interpretation. That he intended to use the psalm to interpret the Gospel is indicated by the fact that at the end of movement 1, after painting his picture of joyful harvesters, he returned to the opening beatitude.

When we turn from the words in movement 1 to the music, we find that the music, like the words, accents the promises of God expressed in lines *b*. This music imparts nothing mournful or doleful, but a mood of quiet assurance and steady confidence. The chorus conveys "shouts of joy" free of triumphalism, a dignity free of pomposity, a solemnity free of portentousness. The biblical words inspired in the composer a choral richness in which a contagious serenity is shared with the audience. The tempo is *lento* to reflect tears, *animáto* to express joy. Though faithful to the words, the music conveys a wealth of feeling that transcends any narrow band of literal thought. The transitions are smooth and steady, the mood deliberate and unhurried, the harmonies rich and intense. In fact, the buoyant cadences that express joy add their own resonance of blessedness to the verbal definition of the Bible. By returning to this musical theme in the postlude of movement 7, the composer places the entire work inside these brackets of blessedness and joy.

Movement 2

The second movement is also grounded in a fusion of Old and New Testament texts, a fusion even more complex than in the first movement. The composer begins by quoting from First Peter, words that the Apostle has quoted from Isaiah:

> "All flesh is like grass
> and all its glory like the flower of grass.
> The grass withers, and the flower falls." (1 Peter 1:24)

Brahms did not adopt the thinking of the Apostle, as suggested by the context in First Peter. He avoided reference to the Christian's rebirth or to the identification of the Word with the good news of Christ (1 Peter 1:23, 25b). Perhaps he found those matters too specifically Christian, too dogmatic in tone, or too resistant to musical invention. Whatever the reason, they did not fit the spirit of the funeral dirge suggested by the metaphor of the grass. The listeners are invited to join a slow, somber march of mourners following a casket to the cemetery, their pace controlled by the roll of the kettledrums. Their grief, however, is not centered on the death of a particular person but on the inescapable withering of "all flesh." In this dirge a musical thinker was reflecting soberly on the universal predicament.

The dirge is soon broken off, however, by a new text from James (5:7), a call to patience that expresses a quite different mood. This call receives musical as well as pictorial embodiment in the image of a farmer who, having planted the seed, waits for the necessary rains. (The denizen of Palestine readily understands the distinction between the early and the later rains.) The music shifts from the *adagio* of the funeral march to the faster *più animáto* in which the falling of the life-giving rain is described in delicate, cascading notes.

> Behold, the farmer waits for the precious fruit of the earth, being patient over it until it receives the early and the late rain.

This idiom of planting and reaping attracts Brahms as it did in the first movement, although there the accent falls upon the promise of joy, and here it falls on the need for patience. By inserting this call for waiting between the lament of Isaiah and the shout of confidence in 1 Peter 1:25, Brahms seems to suggest that the transition between the experience of suffering and the experience of joy is a matter that requires "long patience."

Now, after a brief return to the funeral march, Brahms turns from James to First Peter, completing a sentence that, although complete in the epistle, has been broken off in order to express the sadness of Isaiah and the exhortation of James. The return to First Peter marks a sudden shift in mood, from the reminder of certain death to a triumphal assertion about the endurance of the Lord's word:

> "the grass withers, and the flower falls
> but
> the word of the Lord abides forever."

This surely is one of the most decisive *but*'s in all music. Thought moves from the sober recognition of transience through the summer-long patience of the farmer to the endless patience of God.

What is this enduring word? First Peter suggests one answer; Brahms gives another. This word is the promise given by the Lord to homesick exiles in Isaiah 35:10:

> And the ransomed of the LORD shall return,
>   and come to Zion with singing;
> everlasting joy shall be upon their heads;
>   they shall obtain joy and gladness,
>   and sorrow and sighing shall flee away.

This promise is marked by a rapid acceleration in tempo and a brighter mood. Images of finitude give way to images of eternity (harvest, homecoming, ransomed captives, everlasting joy). The somber tone of the voices at the lower pitches gives way to the exuberant animation of the voices in the higher ranges. The tired pace of pilgrims speeds up as they catch sight of Zion, and their excitement brings the full orchestra into play. At the end the flight of tears is expressed by sharp staccato, and the ascent of the pilgrims to Mount Zion is marked by an ascending line of notes.[11] Jon Bailey observes that here the fugue is used as a means of "playing out" the energies that have been mounting both in verbal text and in musical score.

Movement 3

The text of the third movement is less complicated, for the composer is content to combine four verses from a single psalm with one verse from the Wisdom of Solomon. Again, thought moves from recognizing the ephemeral character of human existence to celebrating the permanent home of righteous souls in the hands of God. A baritone soloist acknowledges death as the nearer horizon, but the chorus replaces that horizon with the wider vistas opened by hope in God.

Note that the opening solo speaks of death in the normal way:

> "LORD, let me know my end,
> and what is the measure of my days." (Ps. 39:4)

Clearly, this voice speaks for all of us as we confront the brevity of life. This prayer of the psalmist, in intimate dialogue with God, elicited a sharp rejoinder from Samuel Butler:

> Of all prayers this is the insanest. . . . "Lord, let me not know mine end" would have been better; only it would be praying for what God has already granted us. . . .
> The prayer is a silly bit of petulance and it would have served the maker of it right to have had it granted.[12]

A very different attitude is expressed by Archibald MacLeish in a letter to a friend who has just discovered that his cancer is terminal:

> It is when one first sees the horizon as an end that one first begins to *see*. . . . Ends are the hardest things in the world to see—precisely because they aren't *things*, they are the end of things. And yet they are wonderful. What would life be without them! . . . if we didn't die there would be no works—not works of art certainly, the only ones that count. . . . Death is the perspective of every great picture ever painted and the underbeat of every measurable poem. . . .[13]

MacLeish's attitude is closer than Butler's to the position of the psalmist, who saw death as a horizon that measured more than months or years. For him death was an image that confronts the finite with the infinite: "In your sight my life-time is as nothing." It is in contrast to God's eternity that "every man goes about as a shadow." In confronting mortality, we confront the possibility that all our troubles, all our turmoil are in vain. We heap up riches, but we know not who will gather them. The words of the baritone solo summarize human transience in all its forms: the brief measure of days, the evanescence of breath, the emptiness of social struggle, the transitory character of wealth. Something of the anguish of Job is caught up in the wistful, poignant, querulous, haunting cry: "And now, LORD, for what do I wait?" (Ps. 39:7). And the music expresses even better than the words the pain embodied in that cry. The music seems to fit words that Brahms himself used in another connection: "Life steals more from one than does death."[14] Like the psalmist, Brahms understood that prayer to the Eternal best expresses all these intimations of mortality. It is in an I-Thou dialogue with the Lord that a believer discovers the fickleness and fragility of all other securities.

The baritone solo ends in a moment of suspense, a musical silence followed by a dramatic answer to the soloist's question: "My hope is in thee." So decisive is the change in tempo, in intonation, in mood, that choruses find it very difficult to sing this triumphal assertion. The difficulties of the singers may correspond to the difficulties that any poet or philosopher faces in juxtaposing a cry that embodies all the agonies of human history and a declaration that articulates the *nevertheless* of human faith in God. What is this faith? For a verbal expression Brahms turns to the Wisdom of Solomon; for a musical expression he composes a lively fugue that imparts both energy and conviction to the confession of faith.

> But the souls of the righteous are in the hand of God,
> and no torment will ever touch them. (Wisd. of Sol. 3:1)

The music gives weight to the conviction that the ultimate horizon of the human spirit is not death, but God. To be sure, prayers to God make the psalmist (and perhaps Brahms) more, rather than less, aware of his own transience. Yet the music underscores the assurance that such transience has lost its power to inflict any great torment on "the souls of the righteous." The musical language adds its own concurrence, for the closing fugue gives a triumphant answer to the prayer, and thereby a ringing resolution to the universal struggle with "vanity."

Movement 4

It is surely no accident that the thought of movement 4 follows immediately upon that of the third. The image of souls in God's hands shifts to the image of dwelling in God's house; the image of the dying petitioner shifts to that of the living God. The four verses of one psalm, voicing a struggle with the shadowy character of life, are followed by three verses of another psalm, voicing songs of joy and praise. Here, at the very center of the *German Requiem,* is a third beatitude, to correspond with the opening (the mourners) and the closing (the deceased) beatitudes. The blessed are the souls now dwelling in God's house.

Neither in the psalm nor in Brahms' thought is the soul's residence, whether in the hands or in the courts of God, a matter to be postponed until after death. The security of the dwelling place is set against the insecurity of accumulated possessions and the frustration of ambitious activity. To be sure, waiting and hoping, longing and fainting, describe ways by which the soul becomes qualified to dwell in God's house, singing his praise. But the loveliness of the dwelling place and the reliability of the hands are basic realities already sustaining the soul that invests its hope only in God.

These texts disclose some of the unexpected and surprising benefits of a full recognition of human mortality. The petition to know the measure of one's days is answered by a new awareness of the loveliness of the house and the blessedness of those who dwell there. This subtle but very important point may explain why movement 4 is the only one of the seven in which the texts Brahms chose do not move dialectically from some kind of suffering to some kind of joy. Often, in the other movements, one text is chosen to express some form of suffering, then a second text is chosen to express some form of joy. Here, the two are fused into one text:

> How lovely is thy dwelling place,
>   O LORD of hosts!
> My soul longs, yea, faints
>   for the courts of the LORD;
> my heart and flesh sing for joy to the
>   living God. (Ps. 84:1–2)

In this crying out of soul and body, Brahms epitomizes first all forms of anguish, then all kinds of joy in the blessedness of those who dwell in the Lord's house, singing his praise. The longing and the singing are not two separate activities, but one. Together they serve to locate the Lord's house and describe what it means to dwell there, thus matching the insight announced in another psalm, that God is "enthroned on the praises of Israel" (Ps. 22:3). The music thus focuses attention not on the transition from death to postmortem life but on the close linkage between the soul's inmost longing and residence in God's dwelling place.

In using Psalm 39, Brahms shows acute awareness of the somber truth of the Syrian proverb "Birth is the messenger of death" and of the

Bulgarian proverb "At birth we cry; at death we see why." But his use of Wisdom of Solomon 3:1 and Psalm 84 shows that Brahms did not bemoan such mortality; rather, he was making a case for it as disclosing a soul-life that cannot be reduced to "the measure of my days." In a recent issue of *The American Scholar,* a similar case is made for recognizing mortality.

> The human soul yearns for, longs for, aspires to some condition, some state, some goal toward which our earthly activities are directed but which cannot be attained during our earthly life. . . . Our distress with mortality is the derivative manifestation of the conflict between the transcendent longings of the soul and the all-too-finite powers and fleshly concerns of the body.[15]

Movement 4 conveys the power of that yearning, the freedom from the slavery to things, and the joy of those who celebrate the loveliness of God's dwelling place. Brahms pictures God as not far away, but always near to the souls whose fearless recognition of mortality is matched by their hope in him.

Movement 5

Two things distinguish movement 5 from the others. It was the last one to be composed, Brahms having added it a month after the Bremen performance of April 1868. Too, this movement is the only one that appears to reflect events in Brahms' own life. One such event was the death of Robert Schumann, Brahms' closest friend. In 1856, going over the manuscripts Schumann left, Brahms came across the title *Ein Deutsches Requiem.* Subsequently he continued to think of the *German Requiem* as belonging to his friend, and the music does retain some motifs and themes reminiscent of Schumann's work. Brahms' continuing grief for his friend may lie beneath the surface of movement 5,[16] but it is more likely that grief at the death of his mother prompted the selection of text and music. She died in 1865; and in 1866, on a trip to her home, he found bits and pieces of music that he had misplaced. Now he set about completing his project.

The movement itself offers evidence of his relationship with his mother.[17] At best, the evidence is circumstantial; but for a musician who was very reticent about revealing his deeper feelings verbally, it is rather convincing. The basic melody is assigned to a soprano soloist, the only movement in the *German Requiem* of which this is true. To be sure, a female soloist is suggested by the metaphor of the mother in the quotation from Isaiah 66:13. But other clues can be found in Brahms' selection of the three texts from three quite disparate writings: the Gospel of John, the prophecy of Isaiah, and the book of Ben Sira (or the Ecclesiasticus of the Old Testament Apocrypha). What led Brahms to these documents in the first place? Why did he give to these three citations meanings so utterly unrelated to their literary contexts? What in his mind linked these fragments? Although no one can speak with assurance, the link may well have been forged by thoughts of his mother.

There is, in fact, a linkage between John 16 and Isaiah 66. Both chapters describe a woman who is giving birth to a child. In Isaiah the image of childbirth is extended to include her suckling the child and dandling the child on her knees, as well as the comfort and joys of later health and strength. In John the verse immediately preceding Brahms' citation develops a similar analogy:

> "When a woman is in travail she has sorrow, because her hour has come; but when she is delivered of the child, she no longer remembers the anguish, for joy that a child is born into the world." (John 16:21)

It is likely that this conjunction of the image of childbirth attracted the composer to John 16:22, which fuses the experiences of suffering and joy, so central to each of the seven movements: "Ye now are sorrowful . . . your heart shall be joyful."

A second conjunction is more than accidental. Brahms' citation from John 16:22 uses a motif found in Isaiah 66:14; immediately following the verse the composer quotes: "You shall see, and your heart shall rejoice." This prophecy was surely in John's mind when he pictured Jesus as saying to his disciples, "You will see me" (repeated three times) and "I will see you again and your hearts will rejoice" (John 16:16–22). The text in the prophet leads directly to the text in the Gospel and to Brahms' use of both in his work.

The texts from Isaiah and John supply the antiphonal structure of movement 5. One antiphon is John 16:22, the soprano solo in which the first-person pronoun is most naturally understood as referring to a mother consoling her bereaved child after her death:

> "So you have sorrow now, but I will see you again and your hearts will rejoice, and no one will take your joy from you."

The other antiphon is Isaiah 66:13, which can best be understood as a choral assurance in which the pronoun *I* is God speaking to the child, recalling the child's memories of the mother's work of giving comfort:

> "As one whom his mother comforts,
> so I will comfort you."

Thus the musical structure expresses the triangular relationship of son, mother, and God.

Now some explanation is needed for the composer's use of the quotation from Ben Sira:

> See with your eyes that I have labored little
> and found for myself much rest. (51:27)

Does the composer think here of his mother speaking? Probably. She had given long years of selfless work, influencing her family in unostentatious ways. Personal memories must have led him to this brief but evocative verse. The movement comes to an end when the most decisive phrases are combined to form a double, interlocking promise—the mother's assurance (you will behold me) and God's confirmation (I will comfort you). This final conjunction denies any final separation or inconsolable grief.

Notice that these three texts cover much of the spectrum of motherhood: pregnancy, childbirth, patient labor, death, comfort in bereavement. This inclusiveness makes it difficult to deny an element of autobiographical recollection. Even so, the personal reference is well hidden; the music itself gives voice to universal, not simply private, emotions. It emphasizes not so much the sense of personal loss as the paradoxical perception of joy in suffering (John), comfort in bereavement (Isaiah), and rest from a life of daily work (Ben Sira).

These biblical texts do not appear, however, in a simple sequence. The composer develops an intricate interchange between soloist and chorus, both parts being sung *espressivo*. At times the chorus augments the melodic line introduced by the mother. At times the chorus replies to the assurance of this mother ("I have found comfort") with the divine promise "I will comfort you."

Movement 6

All three texts in movement 6 are chosen from books of the New Testament and from books that bear upon the mysterious end of all things. This movement continues the thought in movement 4, a result perhaps of the fact that the earliest version contained only six movements and that the treatment of the mother-son motif in movement 5 was a later intrusion. All the scriptural texts chosen for movement 6 are couched in poetic and prophetic idiom, though each illustrates a different literary form: an antithetical couplet from Hebrews, a seer's revelation from First Corinthians, and a doxology from the book of Revelation. The composer gave to each a different musical treatment.

For the opening chorus Brahms had recourse to a brief couplet from the epistle to the Hebrews:

> For here we have no lasting city,
> but we seek the city which is to come. (13:14)

Whatever impulse led the composer to choose this couplet, it is virtually the only verse in the chapter that was germane to his purposes. That chapter defines the *we* as Christians, who seek a city by following Jesus outside the gate, bearing the same abuse he had endured.[18] Presumably Brahms avoided so limited a reference because he wanted his music to speak to a wider audience.

The slow, plodding rhythm of the chorus suggests the trudge of pilgrims, tired yet moving heavily toward the city of their desire. The literary figure of city also suggests that it is not only individuals who are mortal; no permanence exists in their present community, their institutions, their dwelling place, or even their world. What these pilgrims seek transcends any limitation to individual destinies; what is to come, what their souls long for, is a city. Brahms' words and music are so inclusive that they may remind us of the division of humanity into three groups: those who are at home in their own countries but strangers in all other countries; those who are equally at home in all countries; and those who are equally strangers in all countries, including their own. By assuming a degree of universal alienation, the text speaks most forcefully to this third group. This is perhaps the most inclusive image of mortality in the entire work.

When the composer takes up the long quotation from First Corinthians, he changes the mood of the music dramatically. He shifts from chorus to solo and from communal confession to the prophetic disclosure of a heavenly mystery. Speaking for God, the prophet reveals what has hitherto been hidden from his audience—what no eye has seen or ear heard. In response the chorus speaks for the congregation. What is at stake is a mystery about God's house and about life in the "city which is to come."[19]

> We shall not all sleep,
> but we shall all be changed, . . .
> in the twinkling of an eye,
> at the last trumpet.
> For the trumpet will sound,
> and the dead will be raised imperishable.
> and we shall be changed. (1 Cor. 15:51–52)

For the first time in the *German Requiem* the word for death is used, though the prophet is concerned not with the demise of an individual but with death as a universal foe. The composer seems to be intrigued by the image of the twinkling of an eye (that moment at the end of time that cannot be measured in duration) and the blast of a trumpet (the announcement of victory in the cosmic struggle between the primeval foes—death and life).

In traditional requiems a trumpet customarily introduces the *Dies Irae*, the terrors of the final judgment, which all the departed must face and from which deliverance must be sought by the prayers of loved ones.[20] That prospect repelled Brahms. For him the trumpet heralds not the great day of wrath, but the triumph over death seen in its cosmic magnitude. This is a requiem for humankind.

The great climax of this movement is reached in the musical expression of the lines in First Corinthians, which are quotations from Isaiah 25:8 and Hosea 13:14:

> Then shall come to pass what was written:
> "Death is swallowed up in victory."
> "O Death, where is your victory?
> O Death, where is your sting?" (1 Cor. 15:54, 55, author's translation)

By stopping with those lines the composer avoided involvement in the dogmatic connections in Pauline thought between death and sin, between death and the law. He also avoided Paul's explicit linkage of this victory to the death of Jesus.

But Brahms does not treat this victory over death trivially or casually. The music of the struggle and the celebration of victory challenge the skills of the choristers. Death does not surrender easily.

> A savage and exulting chorus mocking at death and hell, calling forth the full power of the chorus, is followed immediately by a broad and radiant C-major fugue, one of the great choral hymns of praise, requiring equal intensity and devotion.[21]

The music of this *Totentanz* mocks at death by a loud emphatic repetition of the single syllable *Wo* (Where?). These staccato questions call attention to God's sharp answer to death's pretensions, to its deceptions, to its claims to have the last word. The human answer to the mocking question is given by the concluding fugue, in which the struggle with death is resolved and the Creator himself is given the glory for the victory. Note, however, that the victory takes the form not of eliminating death from the human story, but of destroying its sting. Its power to create fear, including fear of divine retribution, has been terminated. Death ceases to be in any sense creation's enemy; it is no longer an ominous boundary marked by "no exit" signs but is restored to its ordained place in the Creator's design. The city toward which pilgrims trudge (Heb. 13:14) is the city of singing, where everyone joins in the doxology. The primary focus ceases to fall on the pilgrims' frustration en route and falls instead on the fulfillment of God's creative will.

> "You are worthy, our Lord and God,
> to receive glory and honor and power,
> for you created all things,
> and by your will they existed and were created."
> (Rev. 4:11, author's translation)

This doxology carried a rich cargo of meaning to early Christians, though no one can be sure which of its features attracted Brahms.[22] It is addressed to God, the ultimate Thou, and the music marks the shift from *we* to *you*. In its original context the hymn was sung in heaven by twenty-four elders gathered around God's throne and casting their crowns before the Source of All Glory. But the prophet chose this hymn probably because it was familiar to the churches of Asia; it may therefore be one of the earliest surviving Christian hymns. The ascription of all glory to God implies the refusal to grant similar power to Death, or to anything in the created world. The hymn exemplifies the habit of thinking about the end of all things in a way that corresponds to thinking about the beginning; the architectural symmetry in the doxology imparts a comparable symmetry to human thoughts about the human story. Brahms' selection of such a doxology and his placement of it near the end of the *German Requiem* imparts something of this symmetry to his work. Moreover, the incessant repetition of the fugue at the close of movement 6 may be his way of suggesting that this worship is truly "forever and ever."

Movement 7

> "Blessed are the dead who die in the Lord from now on."
> "Blessed, indeed," says the Spirit, "that they may rest from their labors,
> for their deeds follow them." (Rev. 14:13, author's translation)

In this final text the ultimate concern is not with death as an inanimate thing but with the dead, and the concern is not so much with the dead as with "the Lord." Death becomes a concern when it appears to separate the dead from the living and to separate both from the Lord. In this beatitude the tense is present, not future. God announces a truth, not an uncertain possibility. His announcement is confirmed by the Spirit, speaking through the prophet. The announcement points to the Creator's final judgment on his creation as a whole; it is his verdict on the last day. His blessedness is defined by rest and by the assurance of the fulfillment of "deeds"; by implication, death is viewed as the denial of rest to the weary and as the futility of their deeds.

Why did the composer select this one verse yet ignore its original context, with which he was surely familiar? In the original context the beatitude is limited to those members of the Christian church "who keep the commandments of God and the faith of Jesus" (Rev. 14:12). As I mentioned earlier, Brahms wanted to reach a different and a wider audience. The original context sets the blessing of the faithful against the punishment of "Babylon the great" and all the worshipers of the beast. Brahms wanted nothing to do with the "smoke of their torment" (Rev. 14:8–11). In the Apocalypse, when the Son of man swung his sickle, "blood flowed from the wine press, as high as a horse's bridle" (Rev. 14:14–20). Brahms did not find such a gory picture compatible with his design. The prophet John was writing for a tiny minority of Christians facing death at the hands of a powerful majority. Brahms did not visualize concertgoers in Bremen and Vienna in such terms.

What clues to Brahms' interpretation of this beatitude emerge from his music? The emotional intensity and the sense of full commitment in the music suggest that the composer took the prophetic beatitude with genuine seriousness. The fact that he repeats music from the first movement in the seventh indicates a desire to bind those who die with those who mourn their deaths, and perhaps suggests that this bond, which death always appears to break, is forged by the common bond to God.[23] Clearly the quiet confidence and joy that pervade the closing chorus complete and reinforce the resolution of the conflict that appeared earlier in the recurrent stuggles between transience and permanence, despair and hope. Thus, the final movement of the *German Requiem* is a musical confession of faith that encompasses all the earlier motifs of confidence and comfort. Neither here nor in any earlier movement does the composer allow philosophical debate or theological dogma about death (e.g., what happens to the soul in death) or trivial gossip about life after death (e.g., what kinds of bodies are raised) to intrude upon the consciousness of the audience. His music is a poetry of joy that celebrates the loss of death's sting by drawing the audience into a nonverbal experience of comfort, confidence, and hope.[24]

Indeed, if one were to chart the range of affections experienced by an audience during a performance of the *German Requiem*, one would find a very broad spectrum of responses. They would cover many of the connotations of the term *death*, a term that appears very seldom and only near the end. Brahms was alive to these connotations as they reverberated from the texts. The same may be said about the word *life*, with all its synonyms and surrogates. In fact, that word is usually too narrow to cover all the nuances in Brahms' hymn to joy. In that first decisive *but* he strongly emphasizes the antithesis of human mortality: "But the word of the Lord abides forever." That emphasis, together with the fact that

Brahms restricted himself to texts from the Bible, may well be indicative
of his personal conviction that the Bible itself is the human requiem, its
witness the most solid ground of consolation and the most profitable
source of reflection about mortality.

In short, in the *German Requiem*, human hope rests ultimately in
God; it emerges from his promise to his creation. To dwell in his courts is
the highest activity of the human spirit. To the sorrowing his comfort gives
strength, but such comfort presupposes a sowing in tears and a waiting
with long patience for the harvest. God's beatitude covers the long pil-
grimage of exiles; in the face of the vanity and futility of their ambitions it
assures them that their works follow them. His redemptive grace is not
limited either to life after death or life before death, nor to a select group
of creatures who excel in wisdom, power, or merit. It is not restricted to
members of specific religious institutions; but as God created heaven and
earth, so he redeems the good in all that he has created. Thus Death itself,
conceived of in its mysterious cosmic immensity, has been vanquished
insofar as it threatens humanity, whether the individual who faces it alone
or the race whose mortality is as certain as its life.

✳ ✳

So much for the faith that seems to emanate from the *German
Requiem*, penetrating the subconsciousness of its listeners. But was that
the faith of Brahms himself? No certain answer is possible, chiefly because
of the composer's shyness and his preference for speaking through his music. Some scholars doubt that Brahms shared the basic faith of the biblical
texts, and for that skepticism there is considerable support. Kalbeck, for
instance, reports that in a conversation with Brahms during the year of his
death (1897), the composer said quite openly that neither at the time of
writing the *German Requiem* nor since had he believed in immortality.
The musician indicated that he had tried to avoid any confessional or
creedal emphasis in his desire to speak "to all who believe, irrespective of
creed." And it is true that when Reinthaler urged Brahms to include in
the *German Requiem* some more explicit references to the resurrection of
Christ, he resisted.[25]

The most recent and thorough statement of this skepticism is argued
by Gerber—that in the *German Requiem* the composer was writing not as
a Christian exegete but as a modern artist for whom the end of life brings
only an eternal sleep.[26] Brahms viewed the lovely dwelling place of movement 4 not as reality but as an idyllic dream fantasy. His music expressed
a world-weary piety not unlike that of a contemporary, Friedrich
Nietzsche; his was the resigned voice of a philosophically oriented

thinker.[27] So interpreted, the *German Requiem* becomes a clever but cynical deception of its audiences and a denial of the primary message of the biblical texts.

What should be said of this analysis? This is no place for a full-length rebuttal, but I wish to make several comments. It would be foolish, of course, to require a composer to "believe" all the texts he or she sets to music. The composer stands under no obligation to follow current technical exegesis of the texts or current dogmatic definitions. Brahms' artistic freedom is no more limited than that of the poets who originally constructed these texts. Yet one must say something more than defend Brahms' freedom as a musician. One must try to penetrate the inner integrity of his thought. In this connection, Gerber's analysis illustrates how warped conclusions are guaranteed by posing wrong questions and by working with wrong definitions. Gerber works with nonbiblical definitions of death and life, and therefore thinks in terms of two questions: What happens when doctors pronounce a person dead? Can those bones live again? He insists that Brahms give a verbal answer to those questions within the boundaries set by the definitions. The analyst thus predetermines the answers and limits the options to a simple yes or no. But what happens when those texts presuppose quite different definitions and questions? Those texts perceive death as wearing many masks and taking many forms, and they perceive life, not as an individual's resuscitation from the grave, but as the gift of a loving God. The choice of texts, which was clearly his own act, indicates that Brahms was more at home with those biblical definitions than his critic is. Those texts point away from the simple mortality/immortality option to more imaginative and profound appraisals of the human alternatives:

grief/comfort	sowing/harvesting
exile/homeland	labor/rest
weeping/shouting	earthly cities/heavenly city
despair/hope	aloneness/fellowship
suffering/joy	emptiness/blessedness
stinging death/stingless death	withering/abiding
frustration/fulfillment	defeat/victory

In none of these antitheses does the transition take place simply at the moment of physical death. In all of them the key questions deal not with an individual's demise but with the Creator's purposes for his creation and the creation's participation in those purposes. As a composer, Brahms allowed these texts to speak through his music.[28]

To say that biblical writers addressed death beyond the personal level is not to say that biblical writers were incorrigible optimists, wishful thinkers, who found it easy to move from one pole of these paradoxes to the other. Nor do I mean to say that the composer found that movement easy. Brahms was surely no conventional orthodox theologian, avoiding challenges to complacencies. Yet I find a curious relevance in an observation by Jon D. Bailey, a choral director who has worked many times with the *German Requiem*. In directing choral groups, he has found that their greatest difficulties in mastering the music usually appear at the points of transition, where the composer moves from one mood (e.g., suffering) to its dialectical opposite (e.g., joy). The difficulties of the choruses symbolize the even greater difficulties that most people face in shifting from weeping to shouts of joy. These personal difficulties, in turn, are less acute than those faced by the psalmists and prophets whose texts form the text of the *German Requiem*. So we should not demand of the composer a faith whose strength is measured by yardsticks alien to his own experience. Nor should we be unduly skeptical of the evidence that the Bible played a significant role in that experience.

KRZYSTOF PENDERECKI

St. Luke Passion

THE PASSION AND DEATH OF OUR LORD JESUS CHRIST ACCORDING TO ST. LUKE

Krzysztof Penderecki

Reprinted from Philips recording PHS2-901
by permission of Phonogram International B.V., Baarn, The Netherlands.
Also used by permission of Moeck Verlag.

PART I

I.

O Crux, ave, spes unica,
hoc passionis tempore
piis adauge gratiam
reisque dele, crimina.
Te, fons salutis, Trinitas,
collaudet omnis spiritus.

1. Chorus

Hail, Cross, of hopes the most sublime!
Now in this mournful Passion time
Improve religious souls in grace,
The sins of criminals efface.
Blest Trinity, salvation's spring,
May every soul Thy praises sing.

Roman Breviary (from the hymn
"Vexilla regis prodeunt," Good Friday.)

II.

Et egressus ibat secundum
consuetudinem in Montem
Olivarum. Secuti sunt autem illum
et discipuli. Positis genibus orabat,
dicens:
"Pater, si vis, transfer calicem istum
a me; verumtamen non mea
voluntas, sed tua fiat."

Apparuit autem illi Angelus de coelo
confortans eum. Et factus in agonia,
prolixius orabat. Et factus est sudor
eius sicut guttae sanguinis
decurrentis in terram.

2. Evangelist, Christ

And going out, He went, according
to His custom, to the mount of Olives. And His disciples also followed
Him. And kneeling down, He
prayed. Saying:
"Father, if Thou wilt, remove this
chalice from Me: but yet not My will,
but Thine be done."

And there appeared to Him an angel
from heaven, strengthening Him.
And being in an agony, He prayed the
longer. And His sweat became as
drops of blood, trickling down upon
the ground.

St. Luke 22, 39; 41–44.

III.

Deus meus, Deus meus, respice in me:
quare me dereliquisti?
Deus meus, clamabo per diem, et
non exaudies.

3. Christ's Aria with Chorus

O God, my God, look upon me;
Why hast Thou forsaken me?
O my God, I shall cry by day, and
Thou wilt not hear:

Verba mea auribus percipe, Domine,
intellige clamorem meum.

Give ear, O Lord, to my words:
understand my cry.

Ps. 21 (22), 1–2; Ps. 5, 1.

IV.

Domine, quis habitabit in
tabernaculo tuo,
aut quis requiescet in Monte Sancto tuo?
In pace dormiam et caro mea
requiescet in spe.

4. Soprano Aria

O Lord, who shall dwell in Thy
tabernacle?
Or who shall rest in Thy holy hill?
In peace in the selfsame I will sleep.
Moreover my flesh also shall rest in
hope.

Ps. 14 (15), 1; Ps. 4, 9; Ps. 15 (16), 9.

V.

Adhuc eo loquente, ecce turba: et qui
vocabatur
Judas,
unus de duodecim, antecedebat eos:
et appropinquavit Jesu ut oscularetur
eum.
"Juda, osculo Filium Hominis
tradis?"
"Quasi ad latronem existis cum gladiis
et fustibus: Sed haec est hora vestra
et potestas tenebrarum."

5. Evangelist, Christ, and Chorus

And while He yet spake, behold, a
multitude, and he that was called
Judas,
one of the twelve, went before them,
and drew near unto Jesus, to kiss
Him.
"Judas, betrayest thou the Son of man
with a kiss?"
"Are ye come out, as it were against
a thief, with swords and clubs? But
this is your hour and the power of
darkness."

St. Luke 22, 47–48; 52–53.

VI.

Jerusalem, Jerusalem, convertere ad
Dominum, Deum tuum.

6. Chorus

Jerusalem, Jerusalem, be converted
to the Lord, thy God.

Roman Breviary (Good Friday, First
Nocturn, final versicle to the
Lamentations of Jeremiah.)

VII.

Ut quid, Domine, recessisti longe?

7. Chorus (A Capella)

Why O Lord, hast Thou retired afar
off?

Ps. 9, 22 (Ps. 10, 1 according to the
Hebrew.)

VIII.

Comprehendentes autem eum, duxe-
runt ad domum principis sacerdotum.
Petrus vero sequebatur a longe, quem

8. Evangelist, Servant (Soprano), Peter (Bass), and Chorus

And apprehending Him, they led
Him to the high priest's house. But
Peter followed afar off. But a certain

cum vidisset ancilla quaedam seden-
tem ad lumen, et eum fuisset intuita,
dixit:

"Et hic cum illo erat."
"Mulier, non novi illum"
Et post pusillum alius videns eum,
dixit:
"Et tu de illis es"
"O homo, non sum"
Et intervallo facto quasi horae unius,
alius quidam affirmabat,
dicens:
"Vere et hic cum illo erat, nam et
Galilaeus est."
"Homo, nescio quid dicis."

Et continuo adhuc illo loquente can-
tavit gallus. Et conversus Dominus
respexit Petrum. Recordatus est Pe-
trus verbi Domini et egressus foras
flevit amare.

maid had seen him sitting at the light
and had earnestly beheld him, and
said:

"This man was also with him."
"Woman, I know Him not."
And after a little while, another
seeing him, said:
"Thou also art one of them."
"O man, I am not."
And after a space, as it were of one
hour, another certain man affirmed,
saying:
"Of a truth, this man was also with
him: for he is also a Galilean."
"Man, I know not what thou sayest."

And immediately, as he was yet speaking, the cock crew. And the Lord
turning looked on Peter. And Peter
remembered the word of the Lord.
And going out, he wept bitterly.

St. Luke 22, 54; 56–62.

IX.

Judica me, Deus, et discerne causam
meam.

9. Peter's Aria

Judge me, O God, and distinguish
my cause.

Ps. 42 (43), 1.

X.

Et viri, qui tenebant eum, illudebant
et caedentes: Et velaverunt eum, et
percutiebant faciem eius, et interro-
gabant eum, dicentes:
"Prophetiza, quis est, qui te
percussit?"
"Tu ergo es Filius Deus?"
"Vos dicitis, quia ego sum."

10. Evangelist, Christ, and Chorus

And the men that held Him mocked
Him and struck Him. And they
blindfolded Him and smote His face.
And they asked Him, saying:
"Prophesy: Who is it that struck
thee?"
"Art thou then the Son of God?"
"You say that I am."

St. Luke 22, 63–64; 70.

XI.

Jerusalem, Jerusalem, convertere ad
Dominum, Deum tuum.

11. Soprano

Jerusalem, Jerusalem, be converted
to the Lord, thy God.

Roman Breviary (Good Friday, First
Nocturn, final versicle to the
Lamentations of Jeremiah.)

XII.

Miserere mei, Deus, quoniam concul-
cavit me homo: tota die impugnans
tribulavit me.

12. Chorus (A Cappella)

Have mercy on me, O God, for man
hath trodden me under foot. All day
long he hath afflicted me fighting
against me.

Ps. 55 (56), 2.

XIII.

13. Evangelist, Christ, Pilate
(Bass), and Chorus

Et surgens omnis multitudo eorum,
duxerunt illum ad Pilatum. Coepe-
runt autem accusare illum, dicentes:
"Hunc invenimus subvertentem gen-
tem nostram, et prohibentem tributa
dare Caesari, et dicentem se Chri-
stum regem esse."

And the whole multitude of them,
rising up, led Him to Pilate. And
they began to accuse Him, saying:
"We have found this man perverting
our nation and forbidding to give tribute to Caesar, and saying that he is
Christ the King."

"Tu es rex Judaeorum?"
"Tu dicis."
Nihil invenio causae in hoc homine."
Et remisit eum ad Herodem.
Herodes autem interrogabat illum
multis sermonibus, at ipse nihil illi
respondebat, sprevit autem illum
Herodes indutum veste alba et remisit
ad Pilatum. Pilatus autem convocatis
principibus sacerdotum, dixit ad illos:
"Ecce nihil dignum morte actum est
ei, emendatum illum dimittam."

"Art thou the King of the Jews?"
"Thou sayest it."
"I find no cause in this man."
And he sent Him away to Herod.
Herod questioned Him in many
words. But He answered him nothing. And Herod mocked Him, putting on Him a white garment; and
sent Him back to Pilate. And Pilate,
calling together the chief priests, said
to them: "Behold, nothing deserving
of death has been committed by him.
I will chastise him and release him."

"Tolle hunc, et dimitte nobis Barab-
bam."
Iterum autem Pilatus locutus est ad
illos, volens dimittere Jesum, at illi
succlamabant, dicentes:
"Crucifige, crucifige illum."
"Quid enim mali fecit iste? nullam
causam mortis invenio in eo."
"Crucifige, crucifige illum."

"Away with this man, and release
unto us Barabbas."
And Pilate again spoke to them, de-
siring to release Jesus. But they cried
again, saying:
"Crucify him! Crucify him!"
"Why, what evil hath this man done?
I find no cause of death in him."
"Crucify him! Crucify him!"

St. Luke 23, 1–4; 7; 9; 11; 13; 15–16;
18; 20–22.

PART II

XIV.

14. Chorus

Et in pulverem mortis deduxisti me.

And Thou hast brought me down
into the dust of death.

Ps. 21 (22), 16.

XV.

*Et bajulans sibi crucem, exivit in
eum qui dicitur Calvariae locum, he-
braice autem Golgotha.*

15. Evangelist

And bearing His own cross, He went
forth to that place which is called
Calvary, but in Hebrew Golgotha.

St. John 19, 17.

XVI.

*Popule meus, quid feci tibi?
aut in quo contristavi te?
Responde mihi.
Quia eduxi te de terra Aegypti:*

parasti crucem Salvatori tuo.

*Hagios o Theos, sanctus Deus.
Hagios Ischyros, sanctus Fortis.*

Hagios Athanatos, eleison hemas.

Sanctus Immortalis, miserere nobis.

16. Chorus

My people, what have I done to thee?
Or in what have I grieved thee?
Answer me.
Because I led thee out of the Land of
Egypt,
thou hast prepared a cross for thy
Saviour.

O Holy God, O Holy God,
O Holy, O Mighty One, O Holy, O
Mighty One.
O Holy, Immortal One, have mercy
upon us.
O Holy, Immortal One, have mercy
upon us.

Roman Missal, from the "Improperia"
(Good Friday liturgy.)

XVII.

*Ibi crucifixerunt eum: et latrones,
unum a dextris et alterum a sinistris.*

17. Evangelist

And they crucified Him there: and
the robbers, one on the right hand,
and the other on the left.

St. Luke 23, 33.

XVIII.

*Crux fidelis, inter omnes
arbor una nobilis:
nulla silva talem proferet
fronde, flore, germine:*

*dulce lignum, (dulces clavos)
dulce pondus sustinet.*

*Ecce lignum Crucis,
in quo salus mundi pependit.*

18. Soprano and Chorus

O faithful cross? O noblest tree!
In all our woods there's none like thee!
No earthly groves, no shady bowers
Produce such leaves, such fruits,
such flowers.
(Sweet are the nails) sweet is the wood,
That bears a weight so sweet and good.

Roman Missal, refrain to the hymn
"Pange lingua" (Good Friday liturgy,
veneration of the cross.)

Behold the wood of the cross
on which has hung the Salvation
of the World.

Roman Missal (Good Friday liturgy,
antiphone to the unveiling of the
cross.)

XIX.

Dividentes vero vestimenta eius,
miserunt sortes.
Jesus autem dicebat:
"Pater, dimitte illis, non enim
sciunt, quid faciunt."

XX.

Domine, in pulverem mortis
deduxisti me.
Foderunt manus meas et pedes meos.
Dinumeraverunt omnia ossa mea.
Ipsi vero consideraverunt et
inspexerunt me.

Diviserunt sibi vestimenta mea et
super vestem meam miserunt sortem.

Tu autem, Domine, ne elongaveris
auxilium tuum a me, ad defensionem
meam conspice.

XXI.

Et stabat populus spectans, et
deribebant eum principes cum eis,
dicentes:

"Alios salvos fecit: se salvum faciat,
si hic est Christus Dei electus."

Illudebant autem ei et milites
accedentes, et acetum offerentes ei, et
dicentes.

"Si tu es rex Judaeorum, salvum te
fac."

XXII.

Unus autem de his, qui pendebant,
latronibus, blasphemabat eum,
dicens:
"Si tu es Christus, salvum fac
temetipsum et nos."

19. Evangelist, Christ, and Chorus

But they, dividing His garments, cast
lots.
And Jesus said:
"Father, forgive them, for they know
not what they do."

St. Luke 23, 34.

20. Chorus (A Cappella)

Thou hast brought me down into the
dust of death.
They have dug my hands and feet.
They have numbered all my bones.
And they have looked and stared
upon me.

They parted my garments amongst them,
and upon my vesture they cast lots.
But Thou, O Lord, remove not Thy
help to a distance from me: look
towards my defense.

Ps. 21 (22), 16–20.

21. Evangelist and Chorus

And the people stood beholding.
And the rulers with them derided
Him, saying:

'He saved others: let him save himself,
if he be Christ, the elect of God."

And the soldiers also mocked Him,
coming to Him and offering Him
vinegar, and saying:

"If thou be the king of the Jews, save
thyself."

St. Luke 23, 35–37.

22. Evangelist, the Good Robber (Bass), Christ, and Chorus

And one of these robbers who were
hanged blasphemed Him, saying:

"If thou be Christ, save thyself and
us."

Respondens autem alter increpabat eum, dicens:
"Neque tu times Deum, quod in eadem damnatione es, et nos quidem juste, nam digna factis recipimus; hic vero nihil mali gessit. ›'

"Domine."
"Memento mei, cum veneris in regnum tuum."
"Amen dico tibi: hodie mecum eris in Paradiso."

But the other answering, rebuked Him, saying:
"*Neither dost thou fear God, seeing thou art under the same condemnation? And we indeed justly; for we receive the due reward of our deeds. But this man hath done no evil."*

"Lord!"
"Remember me, when Thou shalt come into Thy kingdom."
"Amen I say to thee: This day thou shalt be with Me in paradise."

St. Luke 23, 39–43.

XXIII.

Stabant autem juxta crucem Jesu mater eius, et soror matris eius, Maria Cleophae, et Maria Magdalene. Cum vidisset ergo Jesus matrem, et discipulum stantem, quem diligebat dicit matri suae:

"Mulier, ecce filius tuus."
deinde dicit discipulo:
"Ecce mater tua."

23. Evangelist, Christ

Now there stood by the cross of Jesus His mother and His mother's sister, Mary of Cleophas, and Mary Magdalen. When Jesus therefore had seen His mother and the disciple standing whom He loved, He saith to His mother:
"Woman, behold thy son."
After that, He saith to the disciple:
"Behold thy mother."

St. John 19, 25–27.

XXIV.

Stabat mater dolorosa
juxta crucem lacrimosa
dum pendebat filius.

Quis est homo, qui non fleret,
matrem Christi si videret
in tanto supplicio.

Eia, Mater, fons amoris,
me sentire vim doloris
fac, ut tecum lugeam.

Fac, ut ardeat cor meum
in amando Christum Deum,
ut sibi complaceam.

Christe, cum sit hinc exire,
da per matrem me venire
ad palmam victoriae.

24. Chorus

At the Cross her station keeping
Stood the mournful Mother weeping,
Close to Jesus to the last.

Is there one who would not weep,
Whelmed in miseries so deep
Christ's dear Mother to behold?

O thou Mother, fount of love,
Touch my spirit from above,
Make my heart with thine accord.

Make me feel as thou hast felt.
Make my soul to glow and melt
With the love of Christ, my Lord.

Christ, when Thou shalt call me hence.
Be Thy Mother my defence.
Be Thy Cross my victory.

Quando corpus morietur,
fac, ut animae donetur
paradisi gloria.

While my body here decays,
Make my soul Thy goodness praise,
Safe in paradise with Thee.

Roman Missal (from the sequence
"Stabat Mater" on the Feast of the
Seven Dolours of Our Lady.)

XXV.

Erat autem fere hora sexta, et tene-
brae factae sunt in universam terram
usque in horam nonam. Et obscura-
tus est sol: et velum templi scissum est
medium. Et clamans voce magna, Je-
sus ait:

"Pater, in manus tuas commendo
spiritum meum."

"Consummatum est."

25. Evangelist, Christ, and Chorus

And it was almost the sixth hour: and
there was darkness over all the earth
until the ninth hour. And the sun was
darkened and the veil of the temple
was rent in the midst. And Jesus
crying with a loud voice, said:

"Father, into Thy hands I commend
My spirit."

"It is consummated."

St. Luke 23, 44–46
and St. John 19, 30.

XXVI.

In pulverem mortis deduxisti me.

Crux fidelis. . . .
Miserere, Deus meus. . . .

In te, Domine, speravi,
non confundar in aleternum:
in justitia tua libera me.
Inclina ad me aurem tuam,
accelera ut eruas me.
esto mihi in Deum protectorem
et in domum refugii, ut salvum me
facias.
In manus tuas commendo spiritum
meum:
Redemisti me, Domine, Deus
veritatis.

26. Chorus and Soloists

Thou hast brought me down into the
dust of death.
Faithful cross. . . .
Have mercy, my God. . . .

In Thee, O Lord, have I hoped,
let me never be confounded;
deliver me in Thy justice.
Bow down Thine ear to me:
make haste to deliver me.
Be Thou unto me a God, a protector,
and a house of refuge, to save me.

Into Thy hands I commend my
spirit:
Thou has redeemed me, O Lord,
the God of truth.

Ps. 30 (31), 2–6.

KRZYSZTOF PENDERECKI
An Interpretation of the Lucan Passion

The youngest composer in the quartet is Krzysztof Penderecki, who was born in 1933, exactly a century after Brahms. The work I shall examine is one of his earlier compositions, the *Passion and Death of our Lord Jesus Christ According to Luke.* This work was commissioned by the West German Radio to celebrate the 700th anniversary of the Münster cathedral, where it was first performed on March 30, 1966.[1] Of his own background, the composer speaks very simply and directly:

> I was raised in a very religious family, and this influenced my life, in living with the Bible which was for me the most important book at that time. Then living in Poland where the religious was forbidden, of course, I wanted to fight against the regime, to make religion important. . . . I believe in God, of course; I couldn't do without it."[2]

Living in Poland, his social consciousness has been deeply affected by many tragic events, which have left their mark on his compositions. The horrors of Auschwitz, not far from Penderecki's hometown, are responsible for his *Dies Irae* (1967); the bombing of Hiroshima is commemorated in his *Threnody* (1960); workers killed in the Gdansk uprising of 1970 are remembered in his *Lacrimosa* (1980); *Kosmogonia* marks the 25th anniversary of the United Nations (1970). Such matters presented challenges at once to the composer's religious faith and to his musical imagination. As Sorab Modi observes:

> The Poland he grew up in and the Poland of today have sharpened his awareness of the human experience at all levels. His religious faith is something very personal, humanistic and ecumenical in the fullest sense.[3]

The quotations from the libretto are from Philips Stereo Recording, PHS2–901.

And the composer himself says:

> I am a Catholic, but membership in a given church is not really the
> point; it is rather that I am very much concerned with these topics . . . in
> an essentially moral and social way, not in either a political or a sectarian
> religious way.[4]

Penderecki admits that Bach and Brahms are among the composers
from whom he has learned most. In the tradition of Passion music he
considers Bach his chief model. When asked why he chose the text of
Luke, he replied, "Stylistically, it's the most beautiful. It has a broad poetic
vision of Christ's suffering. But, also it was one text Bach didn't use. And
I didn't want to offer more ground for comparison than I had to."[5] Another index of Penderecki's respect for the great German Lutheran is his
choice of the musical equivalent of B-A-C-H (B-flat–A–C–B) as the motif
for one or another of the movements in the *St. Luke Passion*.[6] Like Bach,
this musician assigned the words of Jesus to a baritone soloist, but the
words are spoken rather than sung. Like Bach, he used Good Friday liturgical traditions as a frame of reference for the Scripture, though these
traditions for Penderecki were Roman Catholic rather than Lutheran.
Unlike Bach, he wrote for concert hall more than for church, even
though the premiere was performed in a cathedral. Thus his intended
audience was more diverse and his objectives broader than those of Bach.
He has admitted that the *St. Luke Passion* is not altogether a religious
work; in a symbolic way it portrays "through the intolerance shown to one
man the tragedy of all men."[7]

The work calls for an extensive cast: a boys' chorus, three mixed
choruses, vocal soloists, and an orchestra. It is divided into two parts, with
thirteen movements of unequal length in each part. Performance time
requires approximately an hour and twenty minutes. Part 1 covers Luke's
story from Jesus' departure for the Mount of Olives to the sentence of
death (22:39—23:24). It may well be that the first half of the title—*Passion*—is intended to apply to this first part, for it deals with the segment
of the story that accents the anguish in Gethsemane. In part 1, five of the
thirteen movements [3, 4, 7, 9, 12] are drawn from the Psalms, five from
the Gospel [2, 5, 8, 10, 13], and three from the Roman breviary readings
for Good Friday [1, 6, 11]. One of the three from the breviary provides a
literary, theological, and devotional keynote for the whole work:

> Hail, Cross, of hopes the most sublime!
> Now in this mournful Passion time
> Improve religious souls in grace,
> The sins of criminals efface,
> Blest Trinity, salvation's spring,
> May every soul, thy praises sing.

Part 1 ends, after Pilate's announcement of Jesus' innocence, with the horrible cry "Crucify him! Crucify him!"

The thirteen movements in the second part may be intended to represent the noun *death* in Penderecki's double title; it begins with a line from Psalm 22:15, "And thou hast brought me down into the dust of death," and ends in a complex fusion of four sources: (1) that same line from Psalm 22; (2) an ascription to the cross, "Faithful Cross"; (3) a prayer for mercy; and (4) lines from Psalm 31 that include the words Jesus has just spoken from the cross, "Into thy hands I commit my spirit!" (Luke 23:46). Of the movements in this part, seven are drawn from Luke [15, 17, 19, 21, 22, 23, 25]; three from the Psalms [14, 20, 26]; and three from the Roman missal—two from the Good Friday liturgy [16, 18] and the other the extensive hymn *Stabat Mater*, for which Penderecki composed the music separately in 1962 [movement 24].[8] I will discuss first the libretto of these movements and then comment on the musical language.

Verbal Language

The complete text of the *St. Luke Passion* is in Latin. In four lines of movement 16 the Latin is accompanied by its Greek equivalents. The reliance on Latin is rather strange in a work designed for concert audiences whose knowledge of this language is very limited. Moreover, the words are often so submerged in the musical elaboration, so rapidly sung, and so poorly enunciated that the impression is almost inescapable that in the composer's mind the communication of ideas was secondary to the stimulation of feelings. From the same evidence, listeners might infer that the composer was far more experimental and innovative in musical technique than in the conceptual content of the words. This may be a result of Penderecki's Polish Catholic background, which is less known for freedom and diversity in Christian doctrine than for artistic creativity.

The reliance upon Latin may well, however, have better explanations. For one thing, too little time had elapsed for the linguistic liberation achieved at Vatican II to take effect. Moreover, in 1966 it was probably still true that Latin was more universal than either Polish or German, which would have been the other options. Perhaps more important, the use of Latin enables Penderecki to stress the religious "otherness" of Scripture and liturgy. There are both aesthetic and hermeneutic advantages in recognizing the numinous distance that separates any vernacular from the language of redemption. As you will see, Leonard Bernstein's inclination is to move rapidly from the liturgical Latin into the vernacular, diminishing the distance between them, presumably in order to increase the sense of immanence and of relevance. By contrast, Penderecki's use of Latin suggests that the sense of timeless significance may be enhanced by employing more transcendent modalities both in verbal and in musical language.[9]

An examination of the selection of the biblical material yields some surprises. One is the sketchy and eclectic treatment of Luke's Gospel. The title leads listeners to expect a careful and thorough exposition of the Gospel. Most literary analysts would include in the Passion story the whole of chapters 22 and 23, a total of 127 verses; of that total Penderecki uses less than forty percent. This proportion contrasts with the *St. Matthew Passion* of Bach, in which the entire Gospel story, without alteration, was set to music. The Catholic shows less respect for the original document than does the Lutheran. The abbreviation of the story means that many matters that were of significance to the Evangelist have been ignored. Luke included a larger cast of characters and a more extensive series of symbolic episodes than the composer recognized. In writing his Gospel, Luke, like Matthew, had in mind the successors of those early actors—readers who would quickly identify with persons and actions in the story. One gets little impression of this kind of contemporaneity from the segments of Luke that Penderecki chose. Perhaps one reason is the fact that the quotations from Luke constitute a relatively small proportion of Penderecki's total verbal text. Of twenty-six movements, only twelve contain words from Luke, and the interpretation of these fragments is often determined by neighboring citations from other sources. In short, the non-Lucan material overshadows the Lucan. In this respect the title is misleading, except to indicate that of the four scriptural accounts of the death of Jesus, more is drawn from Luke than from the other Gospels.

Another surprise is the number of instances in which Luke's text is supplemented (and sometimes corrected) by material drawn from Mark and John. Although that observation may be of most interest to professional biblical scholars, it does point out some features in the composer's perspective. The first of these additions appears in the third movement, immediately following the account of Jesus' agonized prayer, as his sweat fell like drops of blood (Luke 22:39, 41–44). Penderecki has Jesus sing three prayers, two from Psalm 22 and one from Psalm 5; most strategic are the words "My God, my God, why hast thou forsaken me?" (Mark 15:34). Bible students will immediately recognize that this prayer does not appear at all in Luke, only in Mark (15:34) and Matthew (27:46). Further, when it appears, this "cry of dereliction" is assigned to Jesus on the cross; in Mark it is the only such cry recorded. Assuming, as most scholars do, that Luke used Mark as a major source, he must have intended to omit this cry, not only from the scene of crucifixion but also from the entire record. The reasons for this omission can be known only to Luke, but many readers suspect that it was because the saying reflected a degree of forsakenness and despair on Jesus' part that Luke did not appreciate. Ever since that time, the cry has remained a troublesome problem for many Christian thinkers, though to others it is a positive sign of the full humanity of Jesus and of Mark's respect for a difficult truth. Penderecki's use of the cry represents an editorial revision of Luke. Like the Evangelist, the composer eliminated it from the cries on the cross (the three Lucan cries reflect a very different cluster of moods—Luke 23: 34, 43, 46); unlike Luke, the composer added this cry to the Gethsemane narrative. Presumably he considered it more congenial to that setting; it belonged more to part 1 (the Passion) than to part 2 (the death). In addition, the words of the cry *Deus meus* challenged the musician to produce sounds that would be an unforgettable expression of abysmal agony. In that he succeeded.

A second alteration is even more destructive of Luke's perspective. The Evangelist, following Mark, describes in detail the sad journey from Pilate's courtyard to the Place of the Skull: Jesus' adversaries, probably the Jews, "seized one Simon of Cyrene, who was coming in from the country, and laid on him the cross, to carry it behind Jesus" (Luke 23:26). The Gospel of John paints a very different picture: "he went out, bearing his own cross, to the place called the place of a skull" (John 19:17). It may be true that John knew the Synoptic tradition and chose to correct it for reasons of his own. Whatever we decide on that question, we can be quite certain that Penderecki knew the Lucan version but preferred the Johannine version strongly enough to adopt it [movement 15]. At this point, then, the Passion becomes Johannine rather than Lucan. I am unaware of any written explanation by Penderecki to account for such changes. I infer that they may reflect a cross-mysticism that is more compatible with the picture of Christ bearing the cross alone and that is not interested in the symbol of cross bearing by Simon, which holds implications for later readers, whether disciples or uninvolved passersby.

A still more important deviation from the Gospel of Luke appears in the scene on Golgotha. As Luke describes the death scene, the most important actors, apart from Jesus, are the two criminals, the mocking soldiers, and the centurion. Luke makes a casual reference to the crowd of people watching (23:35) and mentions the fact that "the women who had followed him from Galilee stood at a distance" (Luke 23:49). There is no evidence that Luke included the mother of Jesus among these women; indeed, after a momentary appearance (Luke 8: 19–21), Mary plays no further role in this Gospel. John's portrayal of Golgotha is strikingly differ-

ent (John 19:25–27). In John's text the work of Jesus is not finished until
he makes his final bequest to his mother and to his beloved disciple:

"Woman, behold your son! . . ."
"Behold your mother!"

This is not Luke's Passion story, but John's.[10] Penderecki felt free to make
this change, and he must have felt justified in trying to give a comprehensive account of Jesus' death by drawing on all the Gospels. Yet one infer-
ence is unavoidable—that his addition to Luke in this instance
[movement 23] is due to the Polish Catholic tradition and to the importance of Marian devotion within that tradition.[11]

This addition to Luke enables the composer to introduce into the
next movement [24] six verses from the hymn *Stabat Mater*. The words
of this hymn are as typical of Roman Catholic piety as the words of *O
Sacred Head Now Wounded* are typical of Lutheran piety. In both compositions the memories of the crucifixion are filtered through the images
and cadences of well-loved hymns.

At the Cross her station keeping
Stood the mournful mother weeping,
Close to Jesus to the last.
. . . .

Christ, when thou shalt call me hence
Be thy mother my defence,
Be thy cross my victory.

While my body here decays,
Make my soul thy goodness praise,
Safe in paradise with thee.

Several motifs in this hymn are noticeably absent from the Lucan account: Mary's grief at the cross; her role in defending the believer at the
last judgment; the moment of physical death seen as the separation of soul
from body; salvation seen as admission to paradise after that separation.
The hymn implies that the primary concern of the Gospel is the fate of
the individual soul. It assumes that this fate is dependent upon a person's
devotion both to the Mother and to her Son.

A final addition to the Lucan text is the final utterance from the cross:
"Consummatum est." Drawn from John (19:30), this is a supplement to
the final word in Luke, which for some reason Penderecki found insuffi-
cient. For Luke, the action of the Crucified in committing his spirit to
God was an authentic climax to the story. John wished instead to call
attention to the fact that the mission assigned to Jesus had been completed
on the cross. Basic changes such as these seem to reflect the thrust of
Catholic tradition and of personal piety.

Similar inferences may be drawn from the composer's many deletions from the Lucan story. He includes nothing of the events leading up to the journey to Gethsemane: the conspiracy between the priests and Judas, the arrangements for the Upper Room, the covenant at the Last Supper, the predictions of betrayal, the teaching about greatness and servanthood, instructions about purses and swords (Luke 22:1–38).[12] Also, in the story of Jesus' agony, Penderecki is not interested in Jesus' command to his disciples to stay awake (Luke 22:40, 45–46). He omits the ironic account of the swordplay by which they tried to defend Jesus. Attention focuses on Christ as sufferer, not as teacher of the apprentice Apostles or as a model for their own cross bearing, even though such matters were of vital concern to Luke. One detects a considerable shrinkage in the story of the arrest, the hearing before the priests, and the trial before Pilate. Although Penderecki mentions the crowd's preference for Barabbas, he plays down the culpability of the Jewish antagonists. By omitting Jesus' address to the "daughters of Jerusalem" and the inscription placed over the cross—"the King of the Jews"—Penderecki reveals an indifference to the image of kingship and to the historical reasons for the antipathy between Jesus and the religious and political powers, along with indifference to the possible implications of that hostility for the church as a corporate movement. Instead, he stresses the salvation of the penitent criminal. Typical of his reaction to the story as a whole is the opening prayer: "Improve religious souls in grace." Although this reaction is very common among modern lay people, both Protestant and Catholic, it telescopes the Lucan story into a concern for inner, private experience. We should not, of course, expect from a composer a concern with historical reconstruction or literary criticism. Nevertheless, we need to understand the perspectives from which composers interpret the texts.

One of these perspectives becomes apparent in the psalms Penderecki selected. As I have mentioned, the texts from the psalms are used in eight movements [3, 4, 7, 9, 12, 14, 20, 26] to supplement and to illuminate the Lucan story. In this practice the composer has excellent precedents. Before the Gospels were written and while the stories of Jesus were still circulating in oral form, the only Christian Scriptures were those shared with Israel; and the psalms furnished a central reservoir for Christian worship. Accordingly, as the Passion stories were taking shape, worshipers became aware of many associations between those stories and favorite psalms. One of the Lucan cries from the cross is an example: "Father, into thy hands I commit my spirit!" (Luke (23:46), a direct quotation from Psalm 31. It is altogether probable, therefore, that when these words of Jesus were read in one of Luke's churches, worshipers who were familiar with the psalm would have recalled the entire chapter. Penderecki used precisely that connection. In movement 25 he set to music the cry from the cross; in movement 26 (the final movement) he set to music three verses of Psalm 31 (vss. 1–2, 5). Those verses express a triumphant trust and hope, a reliance on God's justice, and a confident announcement of redemption. All this is Penderecki's expansion of the cry from the cross, but an expansion that is congenial with Luke's intention as voiced in Jesus' final words.

In four movements Penderecki quoted from Psalm 22, which scholars have long recognized as a dominant force in shaping the Passion story while that story was still in its oral stages.[13] In movement 20 several verses from the psalm reverberate in the account of crucifixion: the piercing of hands and feet, the dividing of garments, the casting of lots, the staring and gloating of the soldiers. Penderecki sets those verses to dissonant and strident music. He also brackets the whole of part 2 within one line from this psalm: "thou dost lay me in the dust of death" (Ps. 22:15) [movements 14, 26]. Few summaries could be more succinct. At least three important features in the story are emphasized: the perception of the terrible desolation in this manner of dying, the attribution to God of the underlying responsibility, and the concentration on the I-Thou conversation between Jesus and God as the sole axis of the story's meaning.

Those same features appear in the other quotation from Psalm 22— in movement 3. Here, two lines from the psalm express Jesus' agony in Gethsemane: "My God, my God, look upon me; why hast thou forsaken me? . . . O my God, I cry by day, but thou dost not answer" (Ps. 22: 1– 2). Penderecki does not allow that cry to fade away quickly. Again and again it penetrates the listeners' ears, becoming one of the most haunting and horrible sounds imaginable: *"Deus meus . . . clamabo."* One cannot easily escape the conviction that Penderecki wanted to suggest that Jesus' intense suffering took place in Gethsemane rather than on the cross, that this suffering was inexpressibly and infinitely inclusive in its range and depth, and that somehow the suffering of this one person enclosed the tragedy of all persons. It is in part a tragedy embodied in a cry to God— *clamabo*—a cry that is not answered. Yet the cry, in being addressed to God, assumes that God is able to hear; the psalm bespeaks confidence that all life and all death take place as conversation with a God who hears but who does not intervene to help. As I mentioned earlier, part 1 conveys the composer's understanding of "the Passion . . . of our Lord." That "passion" is telescoped into the cry, in which *domine* is repeated no fewer than eight times and the shrill *clamabo* as often. In the repetition of the cry, Penderecki recognized that the source of Jesus' agony must be traced not only to people but to God. God had sent Jesus on this mission, knowing that in fulfilling it, Jesus would have to bear alone its awful cost. God had been able to hear the cry but had chosen not to reduce that cost. In this sense, God had become an antagonist in Jesus' struggle, and the apocalyptic *clamabo* draws listeners into that same abysmal struggle, a struggle that is at once inescapably real and representative of universal suffering. So the composer's use of Psalm 22 aids him in the interpretation of the Gethsemane episode.

Both Bach and Bernstein relied upon contemporary poets for the librettos to interpret ancient scriptural texts. By contrast, Penderecki selected even more ancient texts as librettos, and in many respects these texts are less foreign to the Passion story, as proved by the fact that they helped to shape that story as it circulated orally in the early churches. In this respect Penderecki follows more closely the practice of Brahms in writing the *German Requiem*.

But what can be said about Penderecki's use of later Catholic liturgy to provide even more strategic perspectives for interpreting Luke [movements 1, 6, 11, 16, 18, 24]? One of these passages [first in movement 6, repeated in movement 11] is drawn from the Good Friday readings in the Roman breviary:

> Jerusalem, Jerusalem, be converted to the Lord thy God.

These words come immediately after the arrest in the Garden and again after the mockery of the soldiers. These events are undoubtedly pivotal ones in the narrative, so the injunction is highly appropriate.

This appeal implies that the story is told to elicit a change in the listeners. They are called to turn toward God and away from alienation. Addressed to Jerusalem, the appeal implies that the audience is more than a chance collection of individuals; it is the elect community, whom God is trying to reach through the events being narrated. The choice of text also implies that the modern audience is to be viewed in some sense as a lineal descendant of the Israel of the Bible. The appeal further implies that the audience, to be true to this heritage, will return to its authentic existence through a repentance induced by the Messiah's suffering. By choosing this verse for his libretto, Penderecki not only uses the liturgy to interpret Luke but also mediates Luke's call to modern audiences. That this act of mediation is not a diversion from Luke's intent is indicated by Jesus' words to "the daughters of Jerusalem," words that Penderecki does not use: "Do not weep for me, but weep for yourselves and for your children" (Luke 23:28).

In using Good Friday readings from the breviary and the missal, Penderecki is, of course, adopting material that is rooted in century-long reflections on the Passion story. That can surely be said of the chorus that immediately follows the account of Jesus' struggling to carry his cross up that final hill [movement 16]. That scene prompts a sharp protest from God, aimed at Israel:

> My people, what have I done to thee?
> Or in what have I grieved thee?
> Answer me!
> Because I led thee out of the land of Egypt,
> thou hast prepared a cross for thy Savior.

In rejecting the Messiah, Israel has rejected God. And the rejection becomes a telescopic summary of Israel's betrayals, beginning with the Exodus,[14] a final gesture of ingratitude and repudiation. For this people's entire history of rebellion, God requires an answer now. The rhetorical questions imply negative answers. God has done nothing to justify these perennial betrayals. The required answer to God's questions emerges in the next lines of the chorus:

> Have mercy upon us.

This climactic prayer appears both in Latin and in Greek. Why? Perhaps to encompass in these two languages the whole span of Christian history. Perhaps to embrace the two largest Christian communions in Poland—the Greek Orthodox and the Roman Catholic. Whatever Penderecki's reason, the use of the two languages accents the response:

> O Holy, Immortal One, have mercy on us.

The prayer for mercy—"kyrie eleison"—has of course been a dominant motif in Christian music from the beginning, so its appearance at this point in the St. Luke Passion is particularly appropriate. Almost immediately thereafter Luke (alone among the Gospels) stresses the words uttered on the cross, "Father, forgive them; for they know not what they do" (23:24). This juxtaposition implies that Israel's prayer for mercy becomes dependent upon the efficacy of Jesus' own prayer. It also brings Israel's prayer into conjunction with that of the penitent thief. This, in turn, associates the salvation assured to the penitent thief with the salvation of the nation.

In movement 18, Penderecki adapts another bit of libretto from the Good Friday liturgy as a comment on the act of crucifixion. In Roman Catholic custom, the cross is veiled on Passion Sunday and unveiled on Good Friday, becoming at that strategic moment a visual object for veneration. This custom is unfamiliar to Protestants, who often find the act of veneration too sentimental and the words a case of misplaced adoration.

> O faithful cross? O noblest tree!
> In all our woods there's none like thee!
> . . . .
> (Sweet are the nails) sweet is the wood
> That bears a weight so sweet and good.

Much may be said in defense of the act of unveiling the cross and accompanying that act with appropriate words and music. Such visualization can help to induce an imaginative recall of the historical event itself. On the other hand, the words and music (e.g., "sweet is the wood") can so romanticize the memories as to separate the event from its horrifying context; Golgotha could not have been further from the ceremonial altar. Whatever our personal reactions, this kind of veneration for the cross has little anchorage in the Gospel of Luke. The veneration implicitly identifies death and salvation with what happened on the cross; it conceives life as an individual's postmortem existence in paradise with Christ and the forgiven thief. As I pointed out in chapter 1, that kind of identification runs counter to the drastic revision in thinking about death and life that characterized early Christianity. Perhaps, then, a musical Passion that begins with the salutation "Hail, Cross" and reaches a climax in the cry "O faithful cross!" [movements 18, 26] distorts the Gospel story by perceiving death in a pre-Christian way.

Musical Language

It should now be clear that the Polish composer has been quite traditional, though also very discerning, in his choice of libretto. He has relied on scriptural texts to tell the story and on ancient liturgical texts to interpret those texts. By contrast, his musical interpretation of those texts demonstrates the highest degree of freedom and innovation. The music is often so expressive that it stimulates great excitement among listeners, yet it is often so disturbing in its novelties that it produces incomprehension and resistance.

> Apart from the work being an extension of Penderecki's religious convictions, the Passion shows how he links the avant-garde trends—hissing, chattering in the voices, and serialism and microtonality—to age-old concepts of music. The result enhances the mood and the theatricality of the score.[15]

Penderecki has been preoccupied from the beginning of his training with the physiology of hearing, particularly the possibility of increasing the human ear's capacity for detecting new sounds. By creating sounds never heard before, he wants to open new channels for tonal communication. He thus places demands on singers to produce sounds that they have never produced before. The soloists in the *St. Luke Passion*, whether soprano or baritone, have very difficult assignments, for which they can no longer rely on mellifluous tones and smooth melodic lines. They are expected to cover an impossible range of sounds and silences that communicate moods that are ominous, numinous, and eerie in the extreme. Dissonances and cacophonies become normal. Heavy use is made of glissandos, quarter tones, and the twelve-tone scale. In fact, the pages of choral music more resemble the terrain maps of ski slopes than the orderly progression of notes on the lines of the staff. Singers must do many things besides sing; they must mutter, jeer, mock, shout—anything to dramatize their participation in the actions of the mobs in Jerusalem. Similar demands are placed on the instrumentalists, who must produce sounds with their violin bows or drumsticks that cannot be represented by the usual musical notations. Penderecki fights shy of the harmonies common to classical Western tradition and prefers the unexpected, unmusical sounds that audience antennae are not accustomed to picking up. To some listeners this extreme range of sounds justifies the quip "Good music isn't nearly so bad as it sounds."[16] The music is not, of course, always bombastic. Some of the shattering blocks of discord, appropriate to mob scenes at criminal executions, are followed by subtle shades of sound more appropriate for intense penitence. Quite apart from the sudden shifts from raucous to pensive tones, the musical language conveys the sense that the subject matter is truly momentous, more momentous than an audience can expect, and even more momentous than can be conveyed by words, however unusual or emphatic. The style is entirely justified by a story filled with deadly conflicts, desolate mourning, excruciating agony, and incredible victory.

> The musical language, notwithstanding its great expressiveness, is severe and constrained, bound by a degree of archaism (notably in the references to the passions of Bach).[17]

The Passion story is of such a character that a composer has full justification in using unconventional techniques. To be sure, the Gospel tells of Jesus' arrest in quite laconic and prosaic terms: "they seized him and led him away" (Luke 22:54). But those terms invite a composer to describe realistically the turbulence of the scene, the shrillness of the voices, the brutal exercise of raw power. Forceful and unrhythmic percussion is entirely in order, just as the wild *sforzando* is suited to the cataclysmic terrors released by this "hour of darkness."[18]

In summing up this analysis of the musical language, one may well ask whether it succeeds in enhancing our understanding of the biblical text and our identification with Luke's audience. The answer must be yes. The music reminds us that the dominant sounds on the first Good Friday were produced not by choirs singing alleluias but by crowds of pilgrims stirred by messianic excitements, by angry mobs aroused to patriotic frenzy, and by soldiers of an occupying army, trying to keep peace in the congested streets of old Jerusalem. The music forces us to leave beautiful sanctuaries and ornate concert halls and to share the tensions and madness of urban demonstrations. It compels us to reenact, however minimally, the violent events that our sacred calendars are designed to commemorate. Penderecki has reminded us that "the tragedy of all men" is somehow present in the intolerance shown to this "one man."

Some of these features appear in specific movements. In movement 1, the composer has prepared the way for the first words of the boys' choir by setting a mood that is mysterious and numinous, prophetically anticipating the whole story.

Hail, Cross, of hopes most sublime.

The music accentuates the inner contradiction that the line contains. How can human hopes be anchored to such an event as a crucifixion? In the Gospel the same contradiction, of course, underlies Jesus' predictions about his coming death.

In the second movement the composer creates a mood appropriate to Jesus' prayer in Gethsemane, "Father, if you will, take this cup from me." Listeners are prodded to feel the full intensity of that prayer. The music carries something of the message found in the diary of Roland de Pury, written in a Paris jail under Nazi occupation: "the place of our captivity, the Biblical place, this abyss of the Psalms, is the spot where Jesus prayed at Gethsemane."[19]

The eighth movement provides a colorful if abrasive background for the interrogation of Peter. The scene in the high priest's house is depicted in such a way that one can sense mounting suspicions and ominous threats. The interchange of accusations and denials is clearly and dramatically portrayed—noisy and confident accusations ("This man also was with him") followed by panicked and overloud denials ("Woman, I do not know him") (Luke 22: 56, 57). Because of the music, the words take on the realism of actual events. Penderecki's audience is linked by the music to Luke's audience.

The last movement in part 1 is the longest and perhaps the most dramatic. The hearing before Pilate is introduced by the hostile mutterings of the mob. In hearing the babble, the jeers, the mocking, one can visualize the crowded scenes, not unlike those painted by Hieronymus

Bosch. The accusations are garbled because of the seething hostility and the implacable fears. His enemies' confusion throws a spotlight on Jesus' fearless reply, "You have said so" (Luke 23:3). Then to Jesus' words the chorus gives a reply that is almost inaudible, a pianissimo confession—"Domine."[20] Pilate repeats his declaration of Jesus' innocence, but the more he tries to free the prisoner, the more stubbornly the crowd calls for the release of Barabbas and the death of Jesus. The Gospel story is so familiar that seldom do readers see what is happening, hear the babble, smell the crowds, feel their emotions, become torn by the tensions, and shudder at the display of brute force. The musical language fosters just that engagement.

In part 2, a smaller proportion of the time is devoted to the Gospel text; a single verse suffices for movements 15, 17, and 19. Much more attention is given to eliciting reflection on succeeding events. One listener has tried to verbalize the gamut of feelings conveyed by this music:

> While listening I forced myself . . . to jot down words which seemed to capture the experience: eerie, tragic, deathly, mysterious, heavy, anguished, desperate, foreboding . . . sinking, falling, wailing . . . harsh . . . fluttering, rushing, whispery, sombre . . . whiney, mocking, groaning, lost, languid . . . descriptive adjectives come relatively easy at the beginning, . . . but in the middle and toward the end words were increasingly difficult. . . . What are we to make of this? The experience of Penderecki's Passion exhausts words. Not only does it exhaust words, but I question whether words are appropriate at all. The language of music . . . is the reservoir of feelings, emotions and experiences which is at once indescribable and still shared between the event and the witness.[21]

I think that those reactions are quite typical of entire audiences who listen to the *St. Luke Passion*. The exorbitance of the composer's musical imagination and the vehemence of his musical language make one recall memories that are deeply etched in the minds and emotions of Penderecki and his contemporaries. One such memory is triggered by the name *Hiroshima*. There is, I think, symbolic significance in Philips' decision to include on the *St. Luke Passion* discs the *Threnody for the Victims of Hiroshima*. Another memory is triggered by the name *Auschwitz* and the names of other concentration camps, which unfortunately have their own descendants today. The associations with such memories discourage us from thinking of the Passion story as so ancient, so limited to ecclesiastical custom, or so familiar that it ceases to be a revelation of a final judgment and a final mercy at those very times when, for us also, the sun is darkened and the veil of the temple is rent [movement 25].

LEONARD BERNSTEIN

Mass

MASS
Leonard Bernstein
and Stephen Schwartz

I. DEVOTIONS BEFORE MASS

1. ANTIPHON: Kyrie Eleison

Quadraphonic tape: From the four corners of the house,
voices enter sequentially.)

Soprano *(Allegretto con spirito)*
Kyrie eleison!   Lord, have mercy!

Bass *(Andante sonore)*
Kyrie eleison!   Lord, have mercy!

Soprano and Alto *(Vivo)*
Christe eleison!   Christ, have mercy!

Tenor and Baritone *(Maestoso)*
Christe eleison!   Christ, have mercy!

(The voices build to a point of maximum confusion, at which a spotlight reveals
a young man, the Celebrant. In his mid-twenties, he is dressed in blue jeans and
a simple shirt. He strikes a strong chord on his guitar which wipes out the sound
from the Quadraphonic tapes.)

2. HYMN AND PSALM: "A Simple Song"

Celebrant (interrupting tape)
Sing God a simple song
Lauda, Laudē . . .
Make it up as you go along
Lauda, Laudē . . .
Sing like you like to sing
God loves all simple things
For God is the simplest of all.

I will sing the Lord a new song
To praise Him, to bless Him, to bless the Lord.

I will sing His praises while I live
All of my days.

Blessed is the man who loves the Lord,
Blessed is the man who praises Him.
Lauda, Lauda, Laudē . . .
And walks in His ways.

I will lift up my eyes
To the hills from whence comes my help
I will lift up my voice to the Lord
Singing *Lauda, Laudē.*

For the Lord is my shade,
Is the shade upon my right hand
And the sun shall not smite me by day
Nor the moon by night . . .
Blessed is the man who loves the Lord—
Lauda, Lauda, Laudē—
And walks in His ways.

(The Celebrant is invested.)

Lauda, Lauda, Laudē
Lauda, Lauda di da di day . . .
All of my days.

3. RESPONSORY: Alleluia

Six solo voices (Quadraphonic tape on four house speakers)
Du bing, du bang, du bong, etc.

Alleluia!
Alleluia! etc.

II. FIRST INTROIT (Rondo)

(The stage is suddenly flooded with people, lights, and music.)

1. PREFATORY PRAYERS

(Street Chorus onstage with marching band)

Street Chorus

Kyrie eleison!	Lord, have mercy!
Christe eleison!	Christ, have mercy!
Gloria Patri et Filio,	Glory be to the Father, and to
Et Spiritui Sancto!	the Son, and to the Holy Ghost!

(Canonically)

Sicut erat in principio	As it was in the beginning,
Et nunc et semper,	Is now and ever shall be,
Et in saecula saeculorum. Amen.	World without end. Amen.

Basses

Introibo ad altare Dei.	I will go up to the altar of God.

Tutti
Ad Deum qui laetificat
juventutem meam.

To God, who gives joy to
my youth.

Women
Asperges me, Domine,
Hyssopo, et mundabor.

Thou shalt sprinkle me with hyssop,
O Lord, and I shall be cleansed.

Two Sopranos
Emitte lucem tuam,
Et veritatem tuam.

Send forth Thy light,
And Thy truth.

Altos
Ostende nobis, Domine

Show us, Lord

Basses
Domine!

Lord!

Altos
Ostende nobis
Misericordiam tuam.

Show us
Thy mercy.

Soprano (gradually joined by others)
Vidi aquam egredientem
De templo latere dextro
Et omnes ad quos pervenit
Aqua ista salvi facti sunt,
Et dicent:

I saw the water issuing from
the right side of the temple
And all those to whom it comes
Are saved by that very water
And say:

Tutti
Alleluia, alleleluiaia! etc.

Alleluia, alleleluiaia! etc.

Boys' Choir (suddenly appearing)
Kyrie eleison!

Lord, have mercy!

Chorus (welcoming them)
Christe eleison!

Christ, have mercy!

Boy (solo)
Here I go up to the altar of God.
In I go, up I go
To God who made me young
To God who made me happy
To God who makes me happy to be young.

(Canonic repeat by Boys' Choir)

2. THRICE-TRIPLE CANON: Dominus Vobiscum

Celebrant
Dominus vobiscum.

God be with you.

Boys' Choir
Et cum spiritu tuo.
All (as a round)
Dominus vobiscum.
Et cum spiritu tuo.

And with Thy spirit.

God be with you.
And with Thy spirit.

III. SECOND INTROIT

1. IN NOMINE PATRIS

Celebrant (speaking over the last fading phrases of the Rondo)
In the name of the Father, and of
the Son, and of the Holy Ghost

Tape (offstage)
In nomine Patris, et Filii, et
Spiritus Sancti, Amen.

(During the preceding music, Acolytes enter the altar space, and the Choir fills
the pews.)

Celebrant (speaking over tape)
Let us rise and pray.

(All rise.)

Celebrant
Almighty Father, bless this house.
And bless and protect all who are assembled in it.

2. PRAYER FOR THE CONGREGATION
   (Chorale: "Almighty Father")

Choir
Almighty Father, incline Thine ear
Bless us and all those who have gathered here
Thine angel send us
Who shall defend us all
And fill with grace
All who dwell in this place.
Amen.

3. EPIPHANY

(Oboe solo on Quadraphonic tape: Sound darting about from all four speakers)

IV. CONFESSION

Celebrant (speakaing over last notes of oboe solo)
I confess to Almighty God,
to blessed Mary ever Virgin,
to blessed Michael the archangel,
to blessed John the Baptist,
to the holy apostles, Peter and Paul . . .

1. CONFITEOR

(Choir and Pit Orchestra overlapping Celebrant's words)

Confiteor Deo omnipotenti,	I confess to Almighty God,
Beatae Mariae, semper Virgini,	To blessed Mary ever Virgin,

Beato Michaeli archangelo,	To blessed Michael the archangel,
Beato Joanni Baptistae,	To blessed John the Baptist,
Sanctis Apostolis Petro	To the holy apostles, Peter
et Paulo,	and Paul,
Omnibus sanctis,	To all the saints,
Et vobis, fratres:	And to you, brothers:
Quia peccavi nimis cogitatione,	That I have sinned exceedingly in
verbo et opere:	thought, word, and deed:
Mea culpa, mea culpa, mea	Through my fault, through my fault,
maxima culpa.	through my own most grievous fault.
Ideo precor beatam Mariam	Therefore I beseech the Blessed
semper Virginem,	Mary ever Virgin,
Beatum Michaelem Archangelum,	Blessed Michael the archangel,
beatum Joannem Baptistam,	blessed John the Baptist,
Sanctos Apostolos Petrum	The holy apostles, Peter
et Paulum,	and Paul,
Omnes sanctos, et vos, fratres,	All the saints, and you, brothers,
Orare pro me	To pray for me
Ad Dominum Deum nostrum.	To the Lord our God.

2. TROPE: "I Don't Know"

Male Street Chorus
Confiteor, Confiteor . . .

First Rock Singer
If I could I'd confess
Good and loud, nice and slow
Get this load off my chest
Yes, but how, Lord—I don't know.

What I say I don't feel
What I feel I don't show
What I show isn't real
What is real, Lord—I don't know,
No, no, no—I don't know.

I don't know why every time
I find a new love I wind up destroying it.
I don't know why I'm
So freaky-minded, I keep on kind of enjoying it—
Why I drift off to sleep
With pledges of deep resolve again,
Then along comes the day
And suddenly they dissolve again—
I don't know . . .

(With descant)
What I say I don't feel
What I feel I don't show
What I show isn't real

What is real, Lord—I don't know,
No, no, no—I don't know.

3. TROPE: "Easy"

First Blues Singer
Well, I went to the holy man and I confessed . . .
Look, I can beat my breast
With the best.
And I'll say almost anything that gets me blessed
Upon request . . .

It's easy to stay as cool as autumn rain
You start by sweeping standards down the well-known drain
Then swap your zeal
For nerves of steel
It's so easy and you feel no pain.

Second Rock Singer
I don't know where to start
There are scars I could show
If I opened my heart
But how far, Lord, but how far can I go?
I don't know.

Second Blues Singer
If you ask me to love you on a bed of spice
Now that might be nice
Once or twice
But don't look for sacraments or sacrifice
They're not worth the price

It's easy to keep the flair in your affair
Your body's always ready, but your soul's not there
Don't be nonplussed
Come love, come lust
It's so easy when you just don't care.

Third Rock Singer
What I need I don't have
What I have I don't own
What I own I don't want
What I want, Lord, I don't know.

Third Blues Singer
If you ask me to sing you verse that's versatile
I'll be glad to beguile you
For a while
But don't look for content beneath the style
Sit back and smile

It's easy to criticize and beat my jive
But hard to deny how neatly I survive
And what could give

More positive
Plain proof that living is easy when you're not alive.

(Simultaneously)
All Three Rock Singers
If I could I'd confess . . .

All Three Blues Singers
Easy . . .

All Three Rock Singers
Good and loud, nice and slow . . .

All Three Blues Singers
Easy . . .

Choir
Beatam Mariam semper Virginem (precor)
Beatum Michaelem Archangelum, beatum Joannem Baptistam,
Sanctos Apostolos Petrum et Paulum,
Omnes sanctos, et vos, fratres,
Orare pro me
Ad Dominum Deum nostrum.

All Six Soloists
What I say I don't feel
What I feel I don't show
What I show isn't real
What is real, Lord—I don't know,
No, no, no—I don't know.

First Rock Singer
Come on, Lord, if you're so great
Show me how, where to go
Show me now—I can't wait
Maybe it's too late,
Lord,
I don't know . . .

First Blues Singer
Confiteor . . .

Celebrant (speaking)
God forgive you.

All (speaking)
God forgive us all.

Celebrant
God be with you.

All
And with your spirit.

Celebrant
Let us pray.

V. MEDITATION # 1 (orchestra alone)

VI. GLORIA

1. GLORIA TIBI

Celebrant
Gloria tibi, Gloria tibi   Glory to You, Glory to You
Gloria!   Glory!

Boys' Choir
Goria tibi, Gloria tibi   Glory to You, Glory to You
Gloria!   Glory!

Celebrant and Boys' Choir (antiphonally)
Gloria Patri,   Glory to the Father,
Gloria Filio,   Glory to the Son,
Et Spiritui Sancto.   And the Holy Ghost.
Laudamus te,   We praise You,
Adoramus te,   We adore You,
Glorificamus te,   We glorify You,
Benedicimus te.   We bless You.

Gloria Patri,   Glory to the Father,
Gloria Filio,   Glory to the Son,
Et Spiritui Sancto.   And the Holy Ghost.
Gloria!   Glory!

Celebrant (speaking)
Glory to God in the Highest and Peace on Earth to Men of Good Will!

2. GLORIA IN EXCELSIS

Choir and Pit Orchestra
Gloria in excelsis Deo,   Glory to God in the highest
et in terra pax hominibus   And on earth peace to men of
bonae voluntatis.   good will.
Laudamus te,   We praise Thee,
Adoramus te,   We adore Thee,
Benedicimus te,   We bless Thee,
Glorificamus te.   We glorify Thee.
Gratias agimus tibi propter   We give Thee thanks for Thy
magnam gloriam tuam: great Glory:
Domine Deus, Rex caelestis,   Lord God, heavenly King,
Deus Pater omnipotens.   God the Almighty Father.
Domine Fili unigenite,   Lord Jesus Christ, only-begotten
Jesu Christe;   Son;
Domine Deus, Agnus Dei,   Lord God, Lamb of God, Son of
Filius Patris: the Father:
Qui tollis peccata   Who takest away the sins of the
mundi,   world,
miserere nobis;   have mercy upon us;
suscipe deprecationem nostram;   Receive our prayer;

Qui sedes ad dexteram Patris,	Thou who sittest at the right hand
miserere nobis.	of the Father, have mercy upon us.
Quoniam tu solus Sanctus,	For Thou alone art the Holy One,
Tu solus Dominus,	Thou alone art Lord,
Tu solus Altissimus:	Thou, Jesus Christ, alone art the
Jesu Christe,	Most High,
Cum Sancto Spiritu: in gloria	With the Holy Ghost, in the glory
Dei Patris. Amen.	of God the Father. Amen.

3. TROPE: "Half of the People"

Street Chorus and Band
Amen!
*Half of the people are stoned
And the other half are waiting for the next election.
Half the people are drowned
And the other half are swimming in the wrong direction.

They call it Glorious Living
They call it Glorious Living
And baby, where does that leave you,
You and your kind—

Choir

. . . *miserere nobis, suscipe*   . . . have mercy upon us, receive
deprecationem nostram . . .   our prayer . . .

Street Chorus and Band
—you and your youth and your mind?
Nowhere, Nowhere, Nowhere.

Half of the people are stoned
And the other half are waiting for the next election—

4. TROPE: "Thank You"

Soprano Solo
There once were days so bright
And nights when every cricket call seemed right
And I sang *Gloria*
Then I sang *Gratias Deo*
I knew a glorious feeling
of thank you and . . .
Thank you . . .

The bend of a willow
A friend and a pillow
A lover whose eyes
Could mirror my cries of *Gloria* . . .

---

*This quatrain was a Christmas present from Paul Simon. Gratias. L.B.

And now, it's strange
Somehow, though nothing much has really changed
I miss the *Gloria*
I don't sing *Gratias Deo*
I can't say quite when it happened
But gone is the . . .
        . . . thank you . . .

Street Chorus
Half the people are drowned, and the other half
Are swimming in the wrong direction.

Celebrant (speaking)
Let us pray.

VII. MEDITATION # 2
(on a sequence by Beethoven, orchestra alone)

(Shortly before the music ends, two altar boys enter, one bearing an elaborate
Bible, the other, a censer. The Celebrant censes the book and kisses it.)

VIII. EPISTLE: "The Word of the Lord"

Celebrant (speaking)
Brothers: This is the gospel I preach; and in its service I have suffered hardship
like a criminal; yea, even unto imprisonment; but there is no imprisoning the
Word of God . . .

A Young Man (as if reading)
Dearly Beloved: Do not be surprised if the world hates you. We who love our
brothers have crossed over to life, but they who do not love, abide in death.
Everyone who hates his brother is a murderer.

Another Young Man (as if reading)
Dear Mom and Dad: . . . Nothing will make me change my mind. Do not feel
badly or worry about me. Try to understand: I am now a man.

Celebrant (singing)
You can lock up the bold men
Go and lock up your bold men
And hold men in tow,
You can stifle all adventure
For a century or so.
Smother hope before it's risen,
Watch it wizen like a gourd,
But you cannot imprison
The Word of the Lord.

Celebrant and Chorus
No, you cannot imprison
The Word of the Lord.

Celebrant
For the Word

For the Word was at the birth of the beginning
It made the heavens and the earth and set them spinning,
And for several million years
It's withstood all our forums and fine ideas
It's been rough
It's been rough but it appears to be winning!

There are people who doubt it
There are people who doubt it and shout it out loud,
There are local vocal yokels who we know collect a crowd.
They can fashion a rebuttal that's as subtle as a sword,
But they're never gonna scuttle the Word of the Lord.

Celebrant and Chorus
No, they're never gonna scuttle the Word of the Lord!

An Older Man (as if reading)
Dear Brothers: . . . I think that God has made us apostles the most abject of mankind. We hunger and thirst, we are naked, we are roughly handled, and we have no fixed abode . . . They curse us and we bless. They persecute us and we suffer it . . . They treat us as the scum of the earth, the dregs of humanity, to this very day.

A Young Girl (as if reading)
Dear Folks: Jim looked very well on my first visit. With his head clean-shaven, he looked about 19 years old. He says the prison food is very good, cafeteria-style. For the first few days he's not allowed any books except his Bible and his breviary. We sat and talked about our marriage and about how we would grow through this. When I hugged him he smelled so good, a smell of clean plain soap; he smelled like a nun, or like a child when you put him to bed.

Celebrant (sung)
All you big men of merit,
all you big men of merit
who ferret out flaws,
you rely on our compliance
with your science and your laws.

Find a freedom to demolish
while you polish some award,
but you cannot abolish
the Word of the Lord.

Celebrant and Chorus
No, you cannot abolish
the Word of the Lord.
For the Word,
for the Word created mud and got it going
It filled our empty brains with blood and set it flowing
And for thousands of regimes
It's endured all our follies and fancy schemes.
It's been tough,
It's been tough, and yet it seems to be growing!

O you people of power,
O you people of power, your hour is now.
You may plan to rule forever, but you never do somehow.

So we wait in silent treason until reason is restored
and we wait for the season of the Word of the Lord.
We await the season of the Word of the Lord.
We wait . . . we wait for the Word of the Lord . . .

IX. GOSPEL-SERMON: "God Said"

Preacher
God said: Let there be light.
And there was light.

Chorus
God said: Let there be night.
And there was night.

Preacher
God said: Let there be day.
And there was day . . .

Chorus
. . . day to follow the night.

Preacher
And it was good, brother

All
And it was good, brother

Preacher
And it was good, brother

All
And it was goddam good.

Preacher
God said: Let there be storms
Storms to bring life . . .

Chorus
. . . life in all of its forms,
Forms such as herds . . .

Preacher
. . . herds and gaggles and swarms
Swarms that have names . . .

Chorus
. . . names and numbers and norms.

Preacher
And it was good, brother

All
And it was good, brother

Preacher
And it was good, brother

All
And it was goddam good!

Preacher
God said: Let there be gnats
Let there be sprats . . .

Chorus
. . . sprats to gobble the gnats
So that the sprats . . .

Preacher
. . . sprats may nourish the rats,
Making them fat . . .

Chorus
. . . fat, fine food for the cats.

Preacher
And they grew fat, brother

All
And they grew fat, brother

Preacher
All but the gnats, brother

All
They all grew fearful fat.

Preacher
And God saw it was good

Chorus
God made it be good

Preacher
Created it good

Chorus
Created the gnats . . .

Preacher
. . . gnats to nourish the sprats . . .

Chorus
. . . sprats to nurture the rats

Preacher
And all for us big fat cats.

All
Us cats!

Chorus
And it was good, and it was good,
And it was good, and it was good.

First Solo (antiphonally with Chorus)
God said it's good to be poor,
Good men must not be secure;
So if we steal from you,
It's just to help you stay pure.

All
And it was good!

Chorus
And it was good! (etc.)

Second Solo (antiphonally with Chorus)
God said take charge of my zoo
I made these creatures for you;
So he won't mind if we
Wipe out a species or two.

All
And it was good!

Chorus
And it was good! (etc.)

Third Solo (antiphonally with Chorus)
God said to spread His commands
To folks in faraway lands;
They may not want us there,
But man it's out of our hands.

All
And it was good!

Chorus
And it was good! (etc.)

Fourth Solo (antiphonally with Chorus)
God said that sex should repulse
Unless it leads to results;
And so we crowd the world
Full of consenting adults.

All
And it was good!

Chorus
And it was good! (etc.)

Fifth Solo (antiphonally with Chorus)
God said it's good to be meek
And so we are once a week;
It may not mean a lot
But oh, it's terribly chic.

All
And it was good!

Chorus
And it was good! (etc.)

Preacher (antiphonally with Chorus)
God made us the boss
God gave us the cross
We turned it into a sword
To spread the Word of the Lord
We use His holy decrees
To do whatever we please

Chorus
Yeah!

Preacher
And it was good!

Chorus
Yeah!

All
And it was good, Yeah!
And it was goddam good!

(The Celebrant suddenly appears among the congregation.)

Preacher (suddenly pious again)
God said: Let there be light.
And there was light.

Chorus
God said: Let there be night.
And there was night.

Preacher
God said: Let there be day.
And there was day . . .

Chorus
. . . day to follow the night.

Preacher
And it was good, brother!

Chorus
And it was good, brother!

Preacher
And it was good, brother!

All
And it was . . .

X. CREDO

Celebrant
I believe in one God, the Father Almighty, maker of heaven and earth, and of all
things visible and invisible. And in one Lord . . . (etc.)

1. CREDO IN UNUM DEUM

(Chorus and percussion on Quadraphonic tape)

Credo in unum Deum, Patrem omnipotentem,	I believe in one God, the Father Almighty,
Factorem caeli et terrae,	Maker of heaven and earth,
Visibilium omnium et invisibilium.	And of all things visible and invisible.
Et in unum Dominum Jesum Christum, Filium Dei unigenitum.	And in one Lord Jesus Christ, the only-begotten Son of God.
Et ex Patre natum ante omnia saecula.	Born of the Father before all ages.
Deum de Deo, lumen de lumine, Deum verum de Deo vero.	God of God, light of light, true God of true God;
Genitum, non factum, consubstantialem Patri:	Begotten, not made, of one essence with the Father:
Per quem omnia facta sunt.	Through whom all things were made.
Qui propter nos homines et propter nostram salutem descendit de caelis.	Who for us men, and for our salvation, came down from heaven.
Et incarnatus est de Spiritu Sancto	And was incarnate by the Holy Ghost
Ex Maria Virgine: et homo factus est.	Of the Virgin Mary: and was made man.

2. TROPE: Non Credo

First Solo (baritone with male vocal group)
(Interrupting tape)

Et homo factus est	And was made man
And was made man . . .	

And you became a man
You, God, chose to become a man
To pay the earth a small social call
I tell you, sir, you never were
A man at all
Why?
You had the choice

When to live
When
To die
And then
Become a god again

Group
And was made man . . .

Solo
And then a plaster god like you
Has the gall to tell me what to do
To become a man
To show my respect on my knees
Go genuflect, but don't expect guarantees
Oh
Just play it dumb
Play it blind
But when
I go
Then
Will I become a god again?

Group
Possibly yes, probably no . . .

Solo
Yes, probably no
Give me a choice
I never had a choice
Or I would have been a simple tree
A barnacle in a silent sea
Anything but what I must be
A man
A man
A man!

Group
Possibly yes, probably no . . .

Solo
You knew what you had to do
You knew why you had to die
You chose to die, and then revive again
You chose, you rose
Alive again
But I
I don't know why
I should live
If only to die
Well, I'm not gonna buy it!

Group
Possibly yes, probably no . . .

Solo
I'll never say credo.
How can anybody say credo?
I want to say cr . . .

(His final word is cut off by the Quadraphonic tape, which continues the *Credo*.)

Tape

Crucifixus etiam pro nobis	He was also crucified for our sake
sub Pontio Pilato,	under Pontius Pilate,
Passus, et sepultus est.	suffered, and was buried.
Et resurrexit tertia die,	And the third day He rose again
secundum Scripturas.	according to the Scriptures.
Et ascendit in caelum:	And He ascended into heaven:
Sedet ad dexteram Patris.	And is seated at the right hand of
Et iterum venturus est	the Father. And He will come again
cum gloria	with glory
judicare vivos et mortuos.	to judge the living and the dead . . .

3. TROPE: "Hurry"

Second Solo (mezzo-soprano)
(Interrupting tape)
You said you'd come again
When?
When things got really rough
So you made us all suffer
While they got a bit rougher
Tougher and tougher
Well, things are tough enough.

So when's your next appearance on the scene?
I'm ready
Hurry
Went to church for clearance and I'm clean
And steady
Hurry
While I'm waiting I can get my bags packed
Flags flown
Shoes blacked
Wings sewn
On . . .

Oh don't you worry—
I could even learn to play the harp
You know it
Show it
Hurry

Hurry and come again.

Tape (interrupting)
Sedet ad dexteram
Patris.
Et iterum venturus est cum gloria
judicare vivos et mortuous:
Cujus regni non erit finis—

He is seated at the right hand of
the Father.
He will come again with glory
to judge the living and the dead:
Whose reign will be without end—

4. TROPE: "World Without End"

Street Chorus (interrupting tape)
Non erit finis . . .
World without end . . .

Third Solo (mezzo-soprano)
Whispers of living, echoes of warning
Phantoms of laughter on the edges of morning
World without end spins endlessly on
Only the men who lived here are gone
Gone on a permanent vacation
Gone to await the next creation

World without end at the end of the world
Lord, don't you know it's the end of the world?
Lord, don't you care if it all ends today?
Sometimes I'd swear that you planned it this way . . .

Dark are the cities, dead is the ocean
Silent and sickly are the remnants of motion
World without end turns mindlessly round
Never a sentry, never a sound
No one to prophesy disaster
No one to help it happen faster
No one to expedite the fall
No one to soil the breeze
No one to oil the seas
No one to anything
No one to anything
No one to anything at all . . .

Tape (interrupting)
Et in Spiritum Sanctum, Dominum
et vivificantem:
Qui ex Patre Filioque
procedit.
Qui cum Patre, et Filio simul
adoratur, et conglorificatur:
Qui locutus est per Prophetas.
Et unam sanctam catholicam et
apostolicam Ecclesiam.
Confiteor unum baptisma in
remissionem peccatorum.
Ex exspecto resurrectionem

I believe also in the Holy Spirit,
Lord and life-giver:
Who proceeds from the Father
and the Son.
Who together with the Father,
and the Son is adored, and glorified:
Who spoke through the prophets.
And I believe in one holy, catholic
and apostolic Church.
I acknowledge one baptism for
the remission of sins.
And I await the resurrection of

mortuorum,   the dead,
Et vitam venturi saeculi.   And the life in the world to come.
Amen.   Amen.

(Simultaneously with the preceding tape, voices overlapping one another)

First Solo
You chose . . . You rose . . .
A man! . . . A man! . . . You chose! . . . You rose! . . .

Second Solo
Hurry and come again . . .
Bags packed, wings sewn, Hurry! . . . Hurry! . . .

Third Solo
World without end, end of the world!
End of the world! Lord, don't you care?
Lord, don't you care?

5. TROPE: "I Believe in God"

Fourth Solo (A Rock Singer, with Street Chorus)
Amen! Amen! Amen! (etc.)

Solo
I believe in God,
But does God believe in me?
I'll believe in any god
If any god there be.
That's a pact. Shake on that. No taking back.

I believe in one God,
But then I believe in three.
I'll believe in twenty gods
If they'll believe in me.
That's a pact. Shake on that. No taking back.

Who created my life?
Made it come to be?
Who accepts this awful
responsibility?

Is there someone out there?
If there is, then who?
Are you listening to this song
I'm singing just for you?

I believe my singing.
Do you believe it too?
I believe each note I sing
But is it getting through?

I believe in F sharp.
I believe in G.
But does it mean a thing to you
Or should I change my key?

How do you like A-flat?
Do you believe in C?—

Choir
Crucifixus etiam pro nobis—

Solo
Do you believe in anything
That has to do with me?

Street Chorus
I believe in God,
But does God believe in me?
I'll believe in thirty gods
If they'll believe in me.
That's a pact. Shake on that. No taking back.

Solo
I'll believe in sugar and spice,
I'll believe in everything nice;
I'll believe in you and you and you
And who . . .
Who'll believe in me?

Celebrant (speaking)
Let us pray.
LET US PRAY!

XI. MEDITATION # 3 (*De Profundis*, part 1)

Choir

De profundis clamavi ad te,	From the depths I cried to you,
Domine;	O Lord;
Domine, audi vocem meam!	Lord, hear my voice!
Fiant aures tuae intentae	Let your ears attend
Ad vocem obsecrationis meae.	The voice of my supplication.
Si delictorum memoriam servaveris,	If you, O Lord, remember only our iniquities,
Domine, Domine, quis sustinebit?	Lord, Lord, who can survive it?.
Sed penes te est peccatorum venia,	But in your hands is the forgiveness of sins,
Ut cum reverentia serviatur tibi.	That you may be served in reverence.
Spero in Dominum;	I trust in the Lord;
Sperat anima mea in verbum eius.	My soul trusts in His word.
Spero! Sperat!	

(Four boys enter carrying sacramental vessels and Sanctus-bell.)

XII. OFFERTORY (*De Profundis*, part 2)

Celebrant (speaking)
Memento, Domine—Remember, O Lord, Thy servants and handmaids . . .[ad lib. names of cast members] . . . and all here present, whose faith is known to

Thee, and for whom we offer up this sacrifice. We beseech Thee in the fellowship
of communion, graciously to accept it and to grant peace to our days.

(The Boys' Choir files in carrying lighted votive candles. The Celebrant blesses
the sacred objects, and leaves the stage.)

Boys' Choir (antiphonally with Choir)

Exspectat anima mea Dominum	My soul waits for the Lord
Magis quam custodes auroram—	More than they who wait for the morning—
Magis quam custodes auroram.	More than they who wait for the morning.
Exspectet Israel Dominum,	Let Israel wait for the Lord,
Quia penes Dominum	For with the Lord is compassion
Misericordia et copiosa penes eum	And with Him is plentiful
redemptio:	redemption:
Et ipse redimet Israel ex	And He will redeem Israel from all
omnibus iniquitatibus eius.	its iniquities.

(A primitive and fetishistic dance around the sacramental objects, interrupted at
a high point by the reappearance of the Celebrant in rich vestments and golden
Cope. All retire in silence.)

XIII. THE LORD'S PRAYER

1. OUR FATHER . . .

Celebrant (alone on stage)
Our Father, who art in heaven
Hallowed be Thy name.
Thy kingdom come
Thy will be done, on earth as it is in heaven.
Give us this day our daily bread
And forgive us our trespasses
As we forgive those who trespass against us.
And lead us not into temptation
But deliver us from evil. Amen.

2. TROPE: "I Go On"

When the thunder rumbles
Now the Age of Gold is dead
And the dreams we've clung to trying to stay young
Have left us parched and old instead . . .
When my courage crumbles
When I feel confused and frail
When my spirit falters on decaying altars
And my illusions fail,

I go on right then.
I go on again.
I go on to say

I will celebrate another day . . .
I go on. . . .

If tomorrow tumbles
And everything I love is gone
I will face regret
All my days, and yet
I will still go on . . . on . . .
Lauda, Lauda, Laudē
Lauda, Lauda di da di day . . .

(Two boys enter with Lavabo-basin. The Celebrant washes his hands.)

XIV. SANCTUS

(The Celebrant seizes the Sanctus-bell and rings it thrice.)

Celebrant (speaking)
Holy!
Holy!
Holy is the Lord God of Hosts! Heaven and earth are full of Thy glory!

Boys' Choir (calling from side to side)
Sanctus, Sanctus, Sanctus	Holy, Holy, Holy
Dominus Deus Sabaoth.	Lord God of Hosts.
Pleni sunt coeli et terra	Heaven and earth are full of
Gloria tuae.	Thy glory.
Osanna, Osanna, Osanna!	Hosanna, Hosanna, Hosanna!

Boys' Choir
Benedictus qui venit in	Blessed is he who comes in the
nomine Domini.	name of the Lord.
Osanna, Osanna, Osanna in	Hosanna, Hosanna, Hosanna in
excelsis!	the highest!
Osanna in excelsis!	Hosanna in the highest!

Celebrant (playing his guitar)
Mi . . . Mi . . .	
Mi alone is only mi.	
But mi with sol	
Me with soul	
Mi sol	
Means a song is beginning	
Is beginning to grow	
Take wing, and rise up singing	
From me and my soul.	
Kadosh! Kadosh! Kadosh!	Holy! Holy! Holy!

(The Chorus begins to enter, in attitudes of gift-offering.)

Choir
Kadosh, Kadosh, Kadosh   Holy! Holy! Holy!
Adonai ts'va-ot   Lord God of Hosts.
M'Lo chol ha-aretz k'vodo   All the heavens and earth are full
                                            of His glory.

(With Street Chorus)
Singing: Holy, Holy, Holy
Lord God of Hosts.
All the heavens and earth
Are full of His glory.

Choir
Kadosh, Kadosh, Kadosh   Holy, Holy, Holy
Adonai ts'va-ot   Lord God of Hosts.
M'Lo chol ha-aretz k'vodo   All the heavens and earth are full
                                            of His glory.

Baruch ha'ba   Blessed is he who comes
B'shem Adonai   In the name of the Lord
B'shem Adonai!   In the name of the Lord!

All voices
Sanctus!   Holy!
Sanctus!   Holy!

(The Celebrant moves to the sacramental objects to begin the consecrations. He
kneels, and as he grasps the Monstrance, he is interrupted by several soloists.)

XV. AGNUS DEI

Male soloists
Agnus Dei,   O Lamb of God,
Agnus Dei, qui tollis peccata mundi,   O Lamb of God, who takest away
                                            the sins of the world

Agnus Dei;   O Lamb of God;
Agnus Dei, qui tollis peccata mundi   O Lamb of God, who takest away
                                            the sins of the world

Miserere, miserere nobis!   Have mercy, have mercy on us!
Miserere, miserere nobis!   Have mercy, have mercy on us!

Male and female soloists
Agnus Dei,
Agnus Dei, qui tollis peccata mundi,
Agnus Dei;
Agnus Dei, qui tollis peccata mundi
Miserere, miserere nobis!
Miserere, miserere nobis!

All soloists and Street Chorus:
Agnus Dei,
Agnus Dei, qui tollis peccata mundi;
Dona nobis pacem!   Give us peace!

Dona nobis pacem!   Give us peace!
Pacem! Pacem!   Peace! Peace!

(The Celebrant grasps the Monstrance and elevates it.)

Celebrant (speaking)
Hoc est enim corpus meum!   This is My Body!

Chorus (men)
Dona . . . nobis . . . pacem . . .

Celebrant (grasping the Chalice)
Hic est enim Calix Sanguinis Mei!   This is the Chalice of My Blood!

Chorus
Dona . . . nobis . . . pacem . . .

Celebrant
Hostiam puram!   Pure Offering!

Chorus (women)
Dona nobis pacem—

Celebrant
Hostiam sanctam . . .   Holy offering . . .

Chorus (women)
Dona nobis pacem—

Celebrant
Hostiam immaculatam . . .   Immaculate offering . . .

Chorus (men)
Dona nobis pacem—

Chorus (women)
Pacem—

Full Chorus
Pacem! Pacem!

Street Chorus plus Choir
Agnus Dei,
Agnus Dei, qui tollis peccata mundi;
Dona nobis pacem!
Dona nobis pacem!
Pacem! Pacem!

(The Celebrant again elevates the Monstrance.)

Celebrant
LET US PRAY!

(The ensemble kneels.)

Choir (women)
Agnus Dei, qui tollis peccata mundi . . .

Choir (men)
Miserere nobis.

(The Celebrant moves to the altar.)

Celebrant
Non sum dignus, Domine.   I am not worthy, Lord.

Choir (women)
Agnus Dei, qui tollis peccata mundi . . .

Choir (men)
Miserere nobis!

(The Celebrant begins to climb the upstage staircase.)

Celebrant
I am not worthy, Lord.

Choir (women)
Agnus Dei, qui tollis peccata mundi!

Choir (men)
Dona nobis pacem!

Celebrant
Corpus! . . .   Body! . . .

Choir
Pacem!

Celebrant (elevating the Chalice)
Calix!   Chalice!

(He continues to climb, with increasing difficulty.)

Choir
Pacem! Pacem!
Dona nobis pacem!

Celebrant
PANEM!   BREAD!

Choir
Dona pacem! Pacem!
Dona nobis pacem!

(The Celebrant reaches the summit. He raises the Monstrance and Chalice. His lips move but no sound emerges. He stands erect, elevating the Monstrance and Chalice above him.)

Choir (the music turning imperceptibly into Blues-stanzas)
Dona nobis, nobis pacem,
Pacem dona, dona nobis,
Nobis pacem, pacem dona,
Dona nobis, nobis pacem,
Pacem dona, dona nobis,

(The stage becomes gradually disorganized. Musicians wander downstage, singers appear where instrumentalists should be, etc.)

Nobis pacem, pacem dona,
Dona nobis, nobis pacem,
Pacem dona, dona nobis,
Nobis pacem, pacem dona,
Dona nobis, nobis pacem,

(The Choir slowly leaves the pews and mixes with the Chorus downstage. The whole stage is in disarray and in turmoil.)

Baritone Solo (gradually joined by five other male soloists)
We're not down on our knees,
We're not praying,
We're not asking you please,
We're just saying:
Give us peace now and peace to hold on to
And God give us some reason to want to
Dona nobis, Dona nobis,

Men
We've got quarrels and qualms and such questions,
Give us answers, not psalms and suggestions.
Give us peace that we don't keep on breaking,
Give us something or we'll just start taking!
Dona nobis, Dona nobis,

All
You worked six days and rested on Sunday.
We can tear the whole mess down in one day.
Give us peace now and we don't mean later.
Don't forget you were once our creator!
Dona nobis, Dona nobis,

We're fed up with your heavenly silence,
And we only get action with violence,
So if we can't have the world we desire,
Lord, we'll have to set this one on fire!
Dona nobis, Dona nobis.

(The preceding stanza is repeated three times, with the constant addition of guitar-improvisations, free obbligati, etc., and ultimately the opening *Kyries* over the Quadraphonic speakers.)

XVI. FRACTION: "Things Get Broken"

Celebrant
PA . . . CEM!
PA . . . CEM!!
PA . . . CEM!!!

(On his last note, he hurls the raised sacraments to the floor. The entire company drops to the floor, where they remain in silence throughout the following.)

Celebrant
Look . . . isn't that—odd . . .
Red wine—isn't red—at all . . .
It's sort of—brown . . . brown and blue . . .
I never noticed that.
What are you staring at?
Haven't you ever seen an accident before?

(He descends the remainder of the steps, picks up a smashed fragment, and smashes it again.)

Look . . . Isn't that—odd . . .
Glass shines—brighter—
When it's—broken . . .
I never noticed that.

How easily things get broken.
How easily things get broken.
Glass—and brown wine—
Thick—like blood . . .
Rich—like honey and blood . . .

Hey—don't you find that funny?
I mean, it's *supposed* to be blood . . .
I mean, it is blood . . . His . . .
It was . . .
How easily things get broken. . . .

What are you staring at?
Haven't you ever seen an accident before?

Come on, come on, admit it,
Confess it was fun—
Wasn't it?
You know it was exciting
To see what I've done.

Come on, you know you loved it.
You're dying for more.
Wasn't it smashing
To see it all come crashing
Right down to the floor!

Right!
You were right, little brothers,
You were right all along.
Little brothers and sisters,
It was I who was wrong—
So earnest, so solemn,
As stiff as a column,
(Parodying himself)

"Lauda, Lauda, Laudē."

Little brothers and sisters,
You were right all along!
It's got to be exciting,
It's got to be strong.

Come on! Come on and join me,
Come join in the fun:

(Defiling the altar)

Shatter and splatter
Pitcher and platter
What do we care?
We won't be there!
What does it matter?
What does it . . .
              . . . matter . . .

Our Father, who art in Heaven,
Haven't you ever seen an accident before?

Listen . . . Isn't that—odd . . .
We can—be—so still . . .
So still and—numb . . .
How easily things get quiet.

Quiet—like a coming storm . . .
Air gets—sickly thick and warm . . .
If I—don't touch the ground,
I might—not make a sound . . .

One, two, three . . .
Soundlessly . . .
Step . . .
Step . . .
Shh . . .
Shh . . .
Softly—as cats can crawl . . .
Almost—not there at all . . .

Carefully . . .
Quietly . . .
Shh . . .

(He reaches the bottom of the steps and lunges at the altar, ripping up the altar
cloths and waving them like streamers in the air. He then leaps up onto the altar
and dances on it.)

Why are you waiting?
Just go on without me
Stop waiting
What is there about me
That you've been respecting

And what have you all been
Expecting to see?

(He tears off his vestments and throws them to the crowd.)
Take a look, there is nothing
But me under this,
There is nothing you'll miss!
Put it on, and you'll see
Any one of you can be
Any one of me!

(He leaps off the altar.)

What?
Are you still waiting?
Still waiting for me,
Me alone,
To sing you into heaven?
Well, you're on your own.

Come on, say it,
What has happened to
All of your vocal powers?
Sing it, pray it,
Where's that mumbo and jumbo
I've heard for hours?

Praying and pouting,
Braying and shouting litanies,
Chanting epistles,
Bouncing your missals
On your knees . . .

Go on whining,
Pining, moaning, intoning,
Groaning obscenities!
Why have you stopped praying?
Stopped your Kyrieing?
Where is your crying and complaining?
Where is your lying and profaning?
Where is your agony?
Where is your malady?
Where is your parody
Of God—said—
Let there be and there was
God said:
Let there *Beatam Mariam semper Virginem,*
Beatam miss the *Gloria,*

I don't sing *Gratias*
Agimus tibi propter magnam

Gloriam tu—am—en . . .
Amen. Amen.

I'm in a hurry—
And come again.
When?
You said you'd come . . .

Come love, come lust,
It's so easy if you just
Don't care—

Lord, don't you care . . .

. . . if it all ends today . . .

. . . *profundis clamavi*
Clamavi ad te,
Domine, ad Dominum,
Ad Dom . . .
. . . A-*donai*—don't know—
I don't no—bis . . .
Miserere nobis . . .

Mi-se . . . mi . . .
Mi alone is only me . . .
But mi with so . . .
Me with s . . . mi . . .

(He sinks to the floor.)

(Like a dirge)

Oh, I suddenly feel every step I've ever taken,
And my legs are lead
And I suddenly see every hand I've ever shaken,
And my arms are dead
I feel every psalm that I've ever sung
Turn to wormwood on my tongue.
And I wonder,
Oh, I wonder,
Was I ever really young?

It's odd how all my body trembles,
Like all this mass
Of glass on the floor.
How fine it would be to rest my head,
And lay me down,
Down in the wine,
Which never was really red . . .
But sort of—brown . . .
And let not—another word—
Be spoken . . .

(He raises himself up onto one arm, slowly stands and begins to descend the pit steps. He pauses at the bottom, leans against the staircase.)

. . . Oh . . .

. . . How easily things get broken.

(He disappears into the pit.)

XVII. PAX: COMMUNION ("Secret Songs")

(After a prolonged silence)

(Flute solo, reprising the "Epiphany")

Boy Soprano
Sing God a secret song
Lauda, Laudē . . .

Lauda, Lauda, Laudē.
Lauda, Lauda, Laudate.
Laudē Deum,
Laudate Eum.

Bass Solo
Lauda, Laudē,
Lauda, Laudē,
Laudē Deum,
Laudē Eum . . .

(They embrace.)

Bass Solo and Boy Soprano
Lauda, Lauda, Laudate . . .

(Two slow chains of embraces begin to form, one originating with the boy, the other with the man.)

First Couple (Soprano and Tenor) in canon:
Lauda, Laudē . . .

Lauda, Lauda, Lauda, Laudē.
Lauda, Lauda, Laudate Deum.
Lauda, Lauda, Laudate Eum.
Laudē Deum, Laudate Eum.

(As the canon continues, they are gradually joined by other couples, eventually by the entire cast. The chains of embraces continue, culminating in a joining of all hands. The Celebrant enters from the side, unobtrusively, and dressed simply, as at the beginning.)

All (whispered in his direction)
Pax tecum!

Boy Soprano and Celebrant
Lauda, etc.

All voices, including stage instrumentalists:
Almighty Father, incline thine ear:
Bless us and all those who have gathered here—
Thine angel send us—
Who shall defend us all;
And fill with grace
All who dwell in this place. Amen.

(The Boys' Choir descends the steps on either side and into the house. The boys fill the aisles, bringing the touch of peace to the audience, saying with each touch, "Pass it on." Their exit coincides with the end of the Chorale.)

Voice on tape:
The Mass is ended; go in Peace.

LEONARD BERNSTEIN
Mass: *A Cry for Peace*

In the work of Bach we listen to an eighteenth-century composer who spent his life in one country, never traveling more than two
hundred miles from his birthplace, and who planned his *St. Matthew
Passion* for small orchestras and choirs in a single church. In the work of
Brahms we listen to a nineteenth-century composer who traveled widely
in Europe, writing the *German Requiem* in at least three different countries (Germany, Austria, Switzerland), and who had access to large choruses in the largest concert halls. In the work of Penderecki we listen to a
twentieth-century composer whose travels take him back and forth from
East zone to West and who is deeply involved both in the musical and the
political upheavals of our time. In Bernstein's *Mass* we listen to a work
composed in cities on three continents (Tel Aviv, Vienna, New York) and
commissioned to inaugurate a center for all the performing arts, named
for an assassinated president.

Nor are these the only contrasts. Note the differences in religious
inheritance: orthodox Lutheran, liberal Protestant, Roman Catholic, Jewish. National origins—German, Polish, American—are obviously important. So, too, are the diversities of musical vocabulary and idiom in
the composers' centuries and cultural traditions. What attracted me to this
quartet, in spite of the contrasts, is their extensive use of Scripture and
their abilities to express in musical language the biblical perceptions of
mortality.

The contrasts among these composers are obvious, but they should
not cause us to forget important similarities. Bernstein, for example, rec-
ognizes a close bond with Bach:

The quotations from the libretto are from Columbia Records, M2–31008.

Once you do get to know Bach well enough to love him, you will love
him more than any other composer. I know this because I went through
the same process myself. For me, Bach meant very little until I was sev-
enteen or so and began to study the *Saint Matthew Passion*. . . . That
glorious work started me off on my own private passion for Bach.[1]

Like Bach, Bernstein used a chorale to express a prayer by and for the
audience. Like Bach, he adopted alternating choruses and orchestras. He
also gave a central place to the sermon and the reading of Scripture; his
recurrent cry of defiance, "You cannot abolish the word of the Lord" bespeaks a profound respect for ancient biblical texts. Like Bach, Bernstein
employed contemporary poetry to interpret those texts, poetry that is often
low-brow rather than high. Both composers often commented on the
same Scripture (e.g., the words spoken at the Last Supper). Both skillfully
adapted secular ditties to sacred uses, employing current musical styles to
stimulate sympathy with ancient traditions, fulfilling the hermeneutical
goal of bridging the chasms of space and time between the Place of the
Skull and the Gothic nave, the theater on the Potomac, or the streets of
New York.

The similarities between Bernstein and Brahms are less marked, the
contrasts more significant. Brahms' work is limited entirely to Scripture;
Bernstein focuses on the Catholic mass and on scriptural segments of that
liturgy. Although the texts Brahms chose reflect many images of mortality,
his musical language remains quite homogeneous in style. Bernstein uses
an even wider range of images of death and an almost unlimited diversity
of musical styles and languages (synagogue chants, medieval chorales,
liturgical Latin, jazz, blues, rock). This diversity can be attributed in part
to the fact that Bernstein was composing for the theater, including actors
and dancers, and in part to his wish to represent all segments of an increasingly cacophonous culture (euphemistically called pluralistic).[2] In
retrospect the Europe of the *German Requiem* seems placid in comparison
with the turbulence of the gestation period of Bernstein's *Mass*. Civil
rights marches and murders, Vietnam protests, Black Panther trials,
flower children, Jesus freaks, the drug culture, Moonies, antinuclear sit-
ins, assassinations—all these find a voice in *Mass*.

Both Brahms and Bernstein give musical expression to the basic paradoxes of biblical faith—suffering and joy, despair and hope. But their
ways of dealing with these antinomies are almost opposite. In successive
movements of the *German Requiem*, both text and music move, as noted
earlier, from a poignant image of mortality toward a heartening pledge of
blessedness. In *Mass* the movement is reversed—from an initial statement
of confident faith, sometimes expressed in traditional creeds and chants,

toward a wave of skeptical, even cynical, rebuttals; and these rejections increase in intensity until the theatrical depiction of death engulfs every singer and actor in a prolonged silence.[3]

It is this uninhibited honesty in *Mass* that so shocks many ecclesiastical authorities, who consider turning the sacrament into theatrical entertainment, inviting pagan ridicule, nothing less than grotesque sacrilege.[4] Yet this very movement from belief to disbelief, a movement that makes the various images of suffering so persuasive, elicits a greater depth of soul searching than does the *German Requiem*. Because all the forms of death are taken more seriously (though at times more humorously), the problem of resolving the tension at the conclusion becomes more complex; but this tension renders the final affirmation of life all the more authentic. Ultimately, Bernstein and Stephen Schwartz (Bernstein's Picander) succeed in turning theatrical entertainment into profound reflection on the diverse perceptions of death and life, enabling listeners to discern anew the original linkage between the Place of the Skull and the sacramental liturgy.[5]

The points of kinship between Penderecki and Bernstein are significant, though more difficult to define precisely. Both give expression to a lively sense of the interaction between religious faith and social conscience, although different events activate that conscience—the events at Auschwitz and Gdansk, for Penderecki, and the emergence of the Black Panthers and the flower children, for Bernstein. Both are aware of the depth of human despair, though one is far more critical of the religious establishment than the other. Both deftly employ highly sophisticated musical language in inventive and imaginative ways. Bernstein's desire for contemporaneity may date his work more quickly and limit future relevance; Penderecki's reliance on ecclesiastical Latin may diminish immediate relevance but secure for his work a longer life. Yet in both works may be detected the cultural cacophonies and violent discords so characteristic of the later decades in the twentieth century.

Turning to a more detailed study of *Mass*, I will present Bernstein's interpretation of the Bible in three stages: how he uses various texts to elicit contemporary skepticisms, how he visualizes different types of mortality, and how he relates the death and resurrection of Jesus to those types. *Mass* was designed as a "theatre piece," an entertainment that was in turn designed to provoke serious reflection on "what it means to live as a religious man in our time."[6]

The Biblical Texts

The Western world is familiar with the song of angels announcing the birth of Christ to Bethlehem shepherds:

"Glory to God in the highest
and on earth peace, good will among men." (Cf. Luke 2:14)

This announcement of peace, with its problem and its promise, links all
the segments of the drama. Where lies the point of contact between the
human cry for peace and this angelic promise? The promise is central in
the segment of eucharistic liturgy called the Gloria. In *Mass* this movement begins with an antiphonal chant of the Gloria Patri, the boys' choir
alternating with the celebrant. Then comes the annunciation from Luke,
confidently declaimed by the celebrant. There follows the Gloria in Excelsis, sung in Latin by the church choir and ending with a solemn *amen*.

Suddenly one hears a sardonic repetition of that *amen* from the street
choir:

Amen!
Half of the people are stoned
And the other half are waiting for the next election.
Half the people are drowned
And the other half are swimming
    in the wrong direction.

The audience is placed in a position to hear both choirs: from the chancel
the Gloria in Excelsis and from the streets "they call it Glorious living,"
though that living gets you "nowhere, nowhere, nowhere." This ribald
antiphon gives way to a solo in a thin soprano voice, the sadness a melan-
cholic contrast to the joy of Luke's angels. Her first verse is a nostalgic
recall of the time when she could sing the Gloria and the *Gratias Deo*; in
her last verse she misses the Gloria and can no longer give thanks. The
wistfulness of the oboe helps the audience realize that the death of God
has eliminated the very possibility of gratitude. The music evokes a dim
sense of grief at God's passing and of the resulting emptiness at the center
of things, an accurate reading of the text of contemporary life.

At this point Penderecki and Bernstein reveal a basic difference in
their approaches to the symbolic relevance of the image of Gethsemane.
To Penderecki the agony of Christ is all-inclusive by reason of its very
uniqueness, Christ's reiterated *clamabo* becomes universally relevant
through its ethereal distance from all other cries. Bernstein's thought, in
contrast, moves in the opposite direction, *from* the specific, if apparently
trivial, heartaches of the passersby on an American street toward the universal inclusiveness of the biblical prayers. So the very absence of gratitude and glory in *Mass* accentuates the relevance of the angel's promise
(Luke 2:14); and the painful contradiction between the messages of the
two choirs creates a provocative context for the call "Let us pray." That

call is followed by an extended period for meditation, which culminates in an orchestral parody of Beethoven's *Hymn to Joy*, the truth and the parody reinforcing each other.

When the period for meditation ceases, the acolytes bring in an elaborate pulpit Bible. After they cense and kiss it, the celebrant begins to read the epistle for the day. In his staging of that reading, the composer treats the Bible as a contemporary document rather than an ancient one.[7] He does not try to change the text to make it more intelligible or relevant. Without any sense of awkwardness the celebrant identifies himself with the apostles, with overtones from Paul:

> Brothers: This is the gospel I preach; and in its service I have suffered hardship like a criminal; yea, even unto imprisonment . . .

He then quotes, from the first letter of John (3:13,15), verses obviously selected and paraphrased to serve as a foil for what follows:

> . . . We who love our brothers have crossed over to life, but they who do not love, abide in death. Everyone who hates his brother is a murderer.

Bernstein illustrates this pivotal biblical definition of life and death by using three speakers whose modern experiences parallel those of early Christians and whose testimonies therefore carry the authority of Scripture. First comes the witness of a young man whose stubborn idealism, contrary to his parents' wishes, has landed him in jail. Then speaks a woman whose husband has been thrown into prison, perhaps because he participated in demonstrations for peace or for civil rights. After her visit to jail she writes his parents about her pride in him and her loyalty to him. The third witness, an older man who bears many scars from altercations with the law, uses Paul's words as if they were his own:

> They curse us and we bless.
> They persecute us and we suffer it. (See 1 Cor. 4:9–13.)

Bernstein thus encourages audiences to accord to such voices the same authority accorded to the Bible and to hear the apostles speak through these victims of American "law and order."

By identifying these "criminals" as heirs of biblical prophets, Bernstein also identifies the heirs of those who persecuted the prophets. "All you big men of merit, . . . you rely on our compliance with your science and your laws. Find a freedom to demolish while you polish some award, . . ." "You can lock up the bold men . . . stifle all adventure for a century or so." But these men "cannot abolish the word of the Lord." So this twentieth-century Jewish composer treats the biblical warfare as contemporary actuality by pointing out the descendants of those who killed the Messiah and his followers. The Passion story then becomes a transcript of current struggles between God's people (redefined) and their enemies (redefined). That Bernstein had the Passion story in mind becomes unmistakable in the announcement to the men of power, "your hour is now," for that is a quotation from the Messiah at the moment of his arrest (Luke 22:53).[8] This kind of direct participation in current political battles was not attempted by either Bach or Brahms.

After reading and expounding the epistle in this way, Bernstein turns to the sermon, which is based on a text from Genesis:

> God said: Let there be light.
> And there was light.
> ....
> And it was good, brother. (See Gen. 1:3–4.)

This text allows the composer to introduce a wide range of funny and satiric responses, so chic in our time. Some of this repartee is relatively playful; for example, the preacher's "It was good" becomes the chorus' "it was goddam good." Other comments are rather grotesque: the goodness of the created gnats, sprats, rats, and cats is proved by one species' becoming fat by consuming another species. This burlesque turns into a savage attack on human society when the cats that grow fat by eating the rats are identified as "us fat cats." That image leads to telling broadsides against the rich who cite Scripture as justification for seeing that the poor stay poor and for protecting the luxuries of the powerful. They use the text of Genesis to rationalize environmental rapacity, which leads to the extinction of one species after another. The following is typical of this savage irony:

> God made us the boss
> God gave us the cross
> We turned it into a sword
> to spread the Word of the Lord
> We use His holy decrees
> To do whatever we please

The sermon on the goodness of creation has become an occasion for proving its perversion. The preacher says "it was good"; in antiphony the chorus jeers cynically, "Yeah!" Because *Mass* makes this cynical attack with full seriousness, albeit with smart-alecky tunes, it may be taken as an attack on religion or an attempt to puncture the self-righteousness of clerics, not unlike biblical protests against hypocrisy and self-deception. Bernstein may be most biblical when he seems most sacrilegious.

Bernstein's treatment of Psalm 130 is quite different. Earlier, I noted how forcefully Penderecki relied on the cry *clamabo* from Psalm 22 in interpreting Jesus' struggle in Gethsemane. In *Mass* Bernstein relied similarly on a line from Psalm 130:

> *De profundis clamavi ad te, Domine.*

It is true that Bernstein does not indulge in any verbal explanation of this cry, but an interpretation is implied by its location and its function in the work. The first four verses, sung in Latin by the choir, serve as a background for prayer. So much of the current unbelief and cynicism precedes the prayer that its words become the expression of the unsatisfied hungers of this ribald congregation. But because of its location, there can be no doubting the sincerity of the cry and no challenge to its relevance. Who can question a poem that so simply and so directly articulates human agony?

> Lord, hear my voice.
> Let your ears attend
> The voice of my supplication.

Such a prayer ignores the centuries that separate the psalmist from the choir of *Mass*. The audience hears only one voice, speaking to one Lord.

The second half of Psalm 130 becomes the text of the offertory, sung antiphonally by the two choirs. The music accompanies the presentation of votive candles and the vesting of the celebrant in preparation for his blessing of the elements. He has spoken a prayer for the actors in the cast and for "peace in our days." No hiatus separates the scriptural antiphons and the twentieth-century petitions. Both merge into a single act of supplication, offering no hint that either the sung or the spoken words are inappropriate.

> My soul waits for the Lord
> More than they who wait for the morning—

By implication, this waiting encompasses all the doubts, denials, and agonies evoked earlier in the work. Because the psalm fits so perfectly into this sequence, it needs no other explication. Later in *Mass* the first line of the psalm is an anguished and irrepressible groan from the celebrant himself as he struggles against despair in his private Gethsemane:

> . . . *profundis clamavi*
> *Clamavi ad te,*
> *Domine.* . . .

For such texts, human suffering provides all the interpretation that is needed.

To summarize the ways in which Bernstein interprets Scripture, I believe that he begins, not with a biblical text, but with contemporary anxieties and injustices, with the Tillichian questions raised by our own existence. For answers, he then selects biblical passages that originally grew out of the same kind of soil so that needs common to both periods may become the preconditons for understanding. He finds present-day spokesmen who, by suffering and courage, have earned the right to relay the authority of prophet or seer; and his audience is one whose needs and questions qualify it to understand its leaders. Some texts elicit skeptical resistance and vigorous rebuttal rather than immediate comprehension or assent. Yet even this response sooner or later helps skeptics to grasp the message, for the biblical text has often emerged out of similar resistance and was intended to defy logical and historical odds. In some texts (e.g., Luke 2:14) the very incredibility of the affirmations, as great in ancient as in modern eras, compels attention, if not respect. Some texts (1 John 3) disclose the perennial recurrences of social conflict between the weak and the strong or moral conflict between popular evil and unpopular good. Still other texts remain always modern because they simply affirm the insoluble character of human problems, inviting listeners to join in a universal *clamavi ad te* and to wait for the morning. For treating diverse texts in these diverse ways, Bernstein belongs among the exegetes whose musical inventions imaginatively link today's audiences and the audiences of the biblical authors. As *Mass* proceeds, the calls to prayer are uttered with mounting desperation, bringing Bernstein's audience into closer and closer kinship with the psalmist.

The Dance of Death

In the segment of *Mass* that is called the confession of sins, Bernstein sounds the first warnings of the struggle with death. As is usual in the liturgy, the celebrant invites the congregation to confess their sins, and this invitation is followed by a Latin chant: *Confiteor Deo omnipotenti.* . . . Breaking roughly into that traditional chant are six soloists, three singing blues and three rock. The words of these solos cover a wide spectrum of needs—from psychic disorientation to sharp cries of guilt. A basic consensus emerges in the confession of a blues singer: "living is easy when you're not alive." Death now wears the mask of easy but empty living. The pathos of this living death finds plaintive expression when the six soloists join in a unison confession:

> What I say I don't feel
> What I feel I don't show
> What I show isn't real
> What is real, Lord—I don't know,
> No, no, no—I don't know.

Such shallow and unreal existence, sad and horrible, encourages the use of current jingles to give voice to spiritual vacuums. The catchy musical idiom becomes a cool form of weeping and wailing, qualifying these confessions for a place in the eucharist. Some of the songs articulate a devil-may-care indifference, but beneath that indifference one senses a yawning abyss: "Come love, come lust. It's so easy when you just don't care." In such plaintive if banal ditties Bernstein has invoked echoes of the narcotized agonies of a whole generation. When he places these songs within the frame of a traditional liturgy, he moves worship out of the chancel into the street; he gives the confiteor a high degree of honesty and depth. To be sure, many of the expressions of guilt are drenched with sentimentality, but that makes them seem all the more genuine. They fulfill the basic function of formal ritual: the sonorous polished phrases of the chant are intended to elicit less polished and less inhibited ejaculations from each individual worshiper. Death is no less real for those whose basic language is limited to bawdy clichés than it is for expert liturgical architects.

When the chancel choir in *Mass* begins to intone the Credo, the responses from the streets are provoked by various clauses in the Nicean formulas, and the typical response takes the form of a *non credo*. Here Bernstein speaks for another segment of his large public, those more sophisticated people who are obsessed with the doctrines they cannot believe. Their recurring antiphon is "Possibly yes, probably no."

The first affirmation that evokes a no is "And was made man." A spokesman from the crowd flatly denies this assertion, on the grounds that Jesus had options that are denied other mortals. When this god chose "to pay the earth a small social call," he could choose when to live and when to die. He knew what he had to do and knew that when it was done he would become a god again. Other men lack such knowledge and such a choice. And so the surly protest: "I tell you, sir, you never were a man at all." One of the oldest of all heresies finds a living spokesman: Jesus' death was not the same death that other men suffer; an unbridgeable chasm yawns between them.[9]

The chasm is widened further by the Credo's affirmation of Jesus' resurrection. That resurrection was supposed to create a bond of solidarity with humankind and to assure our final victory. Instead, it marks a gulf between this one man and all others. Jesus chose to die "and then revive again"; we live only to die. These spokesmen base their *non credo* on the assumption that their understandings of the terms *death* and *life* are adequate. When they rely on those understandings, disbelief is the only honest course. Yet from their disbelief emerges a dim desire to believe:

I'll never say *credo*.
How can anyone say *credo*?
I want to say *cr* . . .

Those three lines call attention to three quite different attitudes that characterize a modern audience, and often all three may be found within a single person. Could they be said more succinctly?

The Credo promises that Jesus will come again; the *non credo* sees only the failure of that promise. The text leaves it uncertain whether the problem lies in Christ's delay or in human impatience. The question "When?" is joined to the demand "Hurry," reflecting the conjunction of suppressed desire for salvation and doubt of its accessibility. The question and the demand echo the cries of early Christians, heard throughout the New Testament. The more intense the suffering, the more insistent the question and the more impatient the demand. Yet both question and demand are met by divine silence; the words do not seem to get through to the other side. Finally the prolonged silence provokes the complaint "Lord, don't you care?"

Again the Credo declares that the world will end in a kingdom without end, a paradox that has baffled the minds of interpreters from the beginning. In the absence of understanding, modern folk cannot be faulted for rejecting such a belief. The world does not end, and the music bemoans the apparent endlessness of an unredeemed world. A dirge begins, nothing less than a wake sung over the corpse of a dead world that goes on forever, turning "mindlessly round." "Dark are the cities, dead is the ocean." The longed-for kingdom of peace does not come, and its absence reveals the cosmic horror of a world rolling endlessly on, as though after a nuclear holocaust. No vision in the book of Revelation is more terrifying. All of earth's people have gone on "a permanent vacation," and a ghastly vacuum remains:

> Silent and sickly are the remnants of motion
>
> . . . .
> Never a sentry, never a sound
> No one to prophesy disaster
> No one to help it happen faster
> No one to expedite the fall
>
> . . . .
> No one to anything
> No one to anything at all . . .

Not surprisingly, Bernstein terminates the struggle between the choir's Credo and the popular *non credo* with a call to prayer, with an orchestral interlude designed to prod listeners to ponder the issues that have emerged. That interlude leads into the urgent petitions of Psalm 130. As I noted earlier, such a sequence makes this psalm as modern as the latest antinuclear demonstration, the futility of which seems all too certain, especially to the demonstrators themselves.[10]

The images of death have emerged in the interpretations of Scripture and the liturgy and in the responses to both. These images derive not alone from the lyrics of Stephen Schwartz, nor alone from the choral and orchestral music, but also from the movements of the dancers and the mimicry of the actors. We must see and hear those dancers and actors as well as listen to their words. At least ten views of death may be distinguished: Death is seen as

> a natural chain of being: "gnats, sprats, rats, cats"
> drug addiction: "half the people are drowned"
> ecological disaster: "wipe out a species or two"
> nuclear extinction: "dark are the cities, dead is the ocean"
> the end of an age: "now the Age of Gold is dead"
> drifting: "living is easy when you're not alive"
> religious colonialism: "we turned it [the cross] into a sword"
> hatred: "they who do not love abide in death"
> martyr's sacrifice: "they persecute us [apostles]"
> a sacrifice of "a god": "you chose to die."

The range of the imagery is wide, but each image has a parallel in the New Testament. Both in Scripture and in modern life, death wears many masks, and many of those masks are the same.

Death and Resurrection

Until the Agnus Dei the types of death remain largely conceptual and reflective. The confiteor has prompted quiet introspection for ferreting out hidden awareness of guilt and frustration. The Credo has released various impulses to skepticism and allowed singers to confess more sophisticated rationalizations of unbelief. Now the Agnus Dei triggers emotions that are volcanic in their suddenness and violence. The movement begins almost routinely, with the Latin chant:

> *Agnus Dei,*
> *. . . qui tollis peccata*
> *mundi,*
> . . . .
> *Miserere, miserere nobis!*

The prayer for pity presumably covers all the implicit and explicit anguish that has been expressed up to this point in *Mass.* But the next petition marks the volcano's eruption:

> *Dona nobis pacem.*

That prayer triggers explosive demands; each word of the celebrant is punctuated by a shrill shout:

Celebrant: This is my body!
Chorus (men):   *Dona . . . nobis . . . pacem.*
Celebrant: This is the Chalice of My Blood!
Chorus: *Dona . . . nobis . . . pacem.*
Celebrant: Pure offering!
Chorus (women):   *Dona nobis pacem—*

The nearer the celebrant approaches the altar, the monstrance in his hand, the more this cry ricochets from all corners of the stage. When the celebrant says *"Panem"* (bread) the worshipers shout *"Pacem"* (peace). The demands from all quarters crescendo as the priest climbs with increasing difficulty toward the high altar. The orderliness of the ritual quickly dissolves into unrestrained turbulence. The audience is no longer watching a churchly service of worship but a huge, uncontrollable public demonstration, with its raucous cries and its shouts of defiance. The protests are leveled both at God and at the celebrant as his human spokesman. The demands are nonnegotiable; if they are not met, vindictive and destructive action is threatened:

You worked six days and rested on Sunday.
We can tear the whole mess down in one day.
Give us peace now and we don't mean later.
Don't forget you were once our creator!
Dona nobis, Dona nobis.

The lyric thus fuses the demand for peace with the threat of vandalism; if hopes prove futile, cosmic destruction will follow. No evasions by priest or deity will be tolerated.

We've got quarrels and qualms and such questions,
Give us answers, not psalms and suggestions.

Through the mounting noise and anarchy, the audience hears this verse repeated three times, fortissimo, by all singers:

We're fed up with your heavenly silence,
And we only get action with violence,
So if we can't have the world we desire,
Lord, we'll have to set this one on fire!
Dona nobis, Dona nobis.

The prayer of the congregation becomes "menacing, wild, barbaric, relentless."[11] Bernstein clearly views this demand for peace, supported by the threat of cosmic suicide, as the most desperate need of our day. Yet there is nothing new about that demand. *Mass* taps an ancient reservoir of pent-up longing, *shalom* in the Old Testament, *eirene* in the New, and *pax* in the eucharistic liturgy. The desire is perennial because, contrary to prophetic pledges, swords are never turned into plowshares. Even so, *Mass* sets that desire to powerful music. Dancers, choruses, soloists, and orchestra join in forcing the audience to feel the volcanic power latent in this perennial frustration.

It is the preacher who feels this tension most acutely. Chosen from among his fellows to serve at the altar, he has found in the words of the psalm a convincing vocation:

> I will sing the Lord a new song
> To praise Him, to bless Him, to bless the Lord.
> I will sing His praises while I live
> All of my days.

He has been vested as celebrant, to the accompaniment of the *lauda*, *laude* and the *alleluia* of his fellows. He has led his congregation in worship and prayer, has read to them the Scripture, and has assured them, "You cannot abolish the Word of the Lord." He has intoned the *Credo* and presented the holy offering. Now, however, his effort to celebrate the communion evokes increasingly raucous demands for peace, uttered against the backdrop of heavenly silence. The turmoil of the streets, the vandalism aroused by God's failure to fulfill his promises, the mounting anarchy—all this finally penetrates his protective subterfuges and impels him to cry, even more desperately than his people, "*Pacem*." With that shout he hurls the sacraments to the floor, shattering the chalice and spilling the wine. His violence actualizes the willful destruction his people have threatened; his desecration of the altar becomes an incarnation of their rebellion: "You were right, little brothers, You were right all along." He confesses how wrong he has been in his earnestness and his distance from his people. Because his vestments have been one symbol of his remoteness, he tears them off. He realizes that his prayers have bypassed the deeper problems of his people and that the celebration of the eucharist has been a way of avoiding the agonies of the world. He has been saying "Peace, Peace" when there has been no peace. Now in his frenzy he utters broken, jagged phrases that echo the earlier cries of his people (e.g., "I don't sing Gratias") and their *non credo*, (e.g., "Lord, don't you care . . . ?"). Even while he is repeating their cries, he accuses them of "whining, pining, moaning, intoning, groaning obscenities!" As his work as a minister has been a parody of the gospel, so, too, their calling as God's people has been filled with lying and self-deception. Their reliance on him as a priest has been as hypocritical as his own pretence of righteousness; their prayers and litanies have been false and their demands a "parody of God." As he repudiates his vocation, the lilting song of joy with which he began his ministry becomes a dirge:

> Oh, I suddenly feel every step I've ever taken,
> And my legs are lead.
> And I suddenly see every hand I've ever shaken,
> And my arms are dead.
> I feel every psalm I've ever sung
> Turn to wormwood on my tongue.
> And I wonder,
> Oh, I wonder,
> Was I ever really young?

The cleric's desecration of sacrament and altar becomes a potent symbol of his death, and his disappearance from the stage makes that death visible: "How easily things get broken."

This staging of the death of the leading actor is much more than a facile theatrical gesture. Coming as it does at the climactic moment, it is associated with the pouring out of the blood of the sacrament. The eucharist does not end here but continues to its normal end in the benediction. The death of the celebrant, linked as it is to the Last Supper, is a vivid reminder of Jesus' struggle in Gethsemane ("Let this cup pass from me") and of his death on Golgotha. Is it entirely coincidental that the entire composition commemorates the assassination of a beloved young president near the auspicious beginning of his presidency?

Not only does the audience watch the gradual unfolding of the Passion story of this young American priest, it also watches as every person on the stage comes to share in that same Passion. At the moment when the celebrant, in despair, shatters the chalice, all other participants drop to the floor, where they remain silent and motionless until the final moments. Pandemonium gives way to silence. In this midnight hour when all souls are unmasked, God is absent; humanity is forsaken; death is king. The Passion story of Jesus is thus revealed in its universal inclusiveness. Bernstein has said that he was interested in depicting the crisis of faith as the central crisis of our time. At the end of this work it becomes apparent that he intended the scene of death on the stage to force the audience to share that crisis, to think about their own faith, or the lack of it, and to ponder the meaning of the cry for peace and the perennial futility of that cry.

Only after a prolonged silence on the stage do sound and movement begin to return. A single flute begins a wistful, thin melody, as if to mark daybreak. The line of melody is taken up by a boy soprano, singing to God a secret song of praise: "*Lauda, laude.*" He touches a prostrate figure, a bass soloist rises to his feet, and the solo becomes a duet. They touch two other "dead" singers, and a tenor and a soprano rise to join in the canon. One by one, two by two, the song of praise awakens the dead, and the dead arise to join in the song until all dancers and actors share in the *lauda, laude.* Unobtrusively the celebrant returns to the stage and is received with the whispered words, *"Pax tecum"*—in sharpest contrast to the earlier shrill demand for peace. With this quiet acceptance of peace, the chorus begins to move from the stage into the aisles of the theater, extending the touch of peace from row to row. Finally the stage is emptied, and the audience is enclosed by the choir. The final words are given:

The Mass is ended; go in Peace.

In this final movement Bernstein has closely associated death with frustrated desires for peace, and resurrection with the gift of peace in a world where there is no peace. He has done both artistic and theological justice to the double truth that the prayer *dona nobis pacem* is forever denied and forever granted. [12] He has identified the efficacy of the sacrament, not with the sacrosanct isolation of bread and wine, but with the sharing of this peace. He has reminded the audience, receiving the touch of peace from the singers, that the gift does not exempt them from sharing in the deaths being endured by neighbors. He has assured those whose faith in God has been destroyed by pious hypocrisies and unending wars (all waged as forms of peacekeeping) that a miraculous gift is still available. [13] *Mass* invites us to broaden our perceptions of death and of life, to discern their presence in surprising places. When we accept that invitation, *Mass* enables us to understand the contemporary relevance of such biblical promises of peace as this:

Peace I leave with you;
my peace I give to you;
not as the world gives
    do I give to you.
Let not your hearts be troubled. . . . (John 14:27)

Postlude

My purpose has not been to compare the works of these four composers or to rate their excellence as interpreters of Scripture, according to some extrinsic standard of greatness. I do, however, wish to point out some of the implications of this study for selected groups of readers. I have in mind three specific groups: biblical exegetes, musicologists, and choirs preparing to sing one of these works.

Professional Exegetes

The task of interpreting Scripture has many dimensions, each of which requires special gifts of the exegete. For example, the exegete must try to recover and reconstruct the series of events that lay behind the literature and prompted its emergence. What really happened? None of the four composers even raised that kind of question, so they are of little help in realizing that goal of the scholar. Another exegetical goal is to express the intellectual concepts to be discerned within the biblical story in order, let us say, to make clearer the doctrinal substance of the Christian faith. In this goal, too, little help can be expected from the musician. Still another important objective is to enhance the modern reader's ability to respond to ancient literature with new appreciations and empathy, to discern overlooked, underground linkages between then and now, to examine current experience through the magnifying glass of archetypal story. In this objective the composer can be of great help. He accepts the story as the ancient writer told it; he follows the narrative line, alert to its subtle nuances; he listens to the overtones of poetic symbolism; he looks beneath the verbal surface of the text for the emotions and moods suggested by the text; he enables his singers to listen to the story afresh and to respond to it with the inner ear. When he is successful, his audience becomes to some degree a part of the audience addressed by the original storyteller, whether

Matthew or Luke or Paul. Once again, an ancient dialogue becomes active in its various dimensions and overtones. Thus the composer reminds the exegete to give full weight to the proper sequence

> before the message . . . the vision,
> before the sermon the hymn,
> before the prose the poem.[1]

The epigram applies not only to modern prose but to ancient documents as well. Before any of the Gospels was written, visions, hymns, and poems circulating within the early church gave both substance and style to the story of Jesus' life and death. Thus, by listening to the musical testimonies of great composers, exegetes may come closer to the infrastructure of literary tradition. Alleluias and amens lie on the other side, as well as on this side, of the Matthean and Lucan Passions.

Exegetes have recently become almost obsessed with the insolubility of the hermeneutical problem, sensing that the cultural distances between ancient texts and modern readers are too immense to be bridged. That is one obsession the composers have not shared. They set the ancient story to music as if it were fully contemporary and readily intelligible, and their listeners often give ample evidence of the composers' success. This success is accomplished in part by supplying the emotional and affectional ambience out of which the texts were born or which they were designed to produce. This ambience is especially true of the human experiences of dying. Death is the same in every century and on every continent. Biblical thinking about death is different from nonbiblical thinking, but the difference is more experiential than temporal. Composers who set death to music can therefore help exegetes grasp the transtemporal and transcultural range of meanings in the crucifixion of Jesus and in subsequent stories of that death. What Walt Whitman said about music applies equally to these stories, and exegetes would do well to heed him:

All music is what awakes from you when you are reminded by the instruments,
It is not the violins and the cornets, it is not the oboe nor the beating drums,
    nor the score of the baritone singer . . . nor that of the men's chorus . . .
It is nearer and farther than they.[2]

It is not the Gospel story, but what awakes within you when you listen to it. The musician can help the exegete become aware of what awakes. For example, if I may compare typical scholarly comments on the Gethsemane episode with Penderecki's musical interpretation of that episode, the composer may have done greater justice to the explosive hatreds and messianic excitements implicit in that story. He has heard its cosmic reverberations.

Musicologists

At the outset I noted that Albert Schweitzer was probably the most recent musicologist whose study of J. S. Bach was informed to some degree by his professional study of Scripture. The great Parisian organist Charles Widor tells of an incident in 1899 when he and Schweitzer were going through some of Bach's chorale preludes. Widor commented that the chorale melodies seemed very cloudy and enigmatic. Schweitzer replied that the obscurity was due to Widor's ignorance of the chorale texts. When Schweitzer translated those texts, Widor tells us, the "mysteries were all solved. . . . I made the acquaintance of a Bach of whose existence I had previously had only the dimmest suspicion."[3]

I hazard the guess that many musicologists share Widor's situation. When they study the work of a composer who has set a biblical text to music, they pay too little attention to some of the links in the chain of composition: the verbal shape and thrust of the biblical verses, the inner response of the composer to those verses, and the musical language by which the composer conveys that response. One of those links may dominate the resulting work, but all three are present to some degree. No scholar, conducting an autopsy on the music, can trace this chain back to its earliest impulses nor speak confidently of the efforts to do so. If, however, musicologists ignore the biblical text and reverberations it awakens in its readers, the analysis of the resulting music will be faulty. Or if a musicologist moves directly from the verbal text of the Bible to the composition itself, ignoring the composer's inner, human responses to that text, the analysis will not do justice to the composer as a person. Musicologists are under a strong obligation to honor composers by doing justice to all stages in the gestation of a work. To be sure, the intentional fallacy can be present; but to be wholly insensitive to the intentions of the biblical text or to the response of the composer is to do violence both to the two persons involved and to their music. If the chasm between the two disciplines—exegesis and musicology—is to be bridged, craftsmen will be needed to work from opposite banks.

Singers

Considered numerically, more chorus members and directors work directly with these works than do either musicologists or professional biblical exegetes. I hope that this study will convince them of the value of analyzing the libretto of a work before they sing it or direct it. As composers are in some sense the servants of the biblical story being interpreted, so performers are in some sense the servants of the interpreter. As the composers have shaped musical language to convey their responses to the story, so musicians must convey a double response to that story, their own and the composer's. I concede "that an audience of average musical level takes remarkably little notice of the text." In one test of audience reactions, only six percent of the listeners were aware that the words of the text made no sense whatever.[4] But when a composer has selected the words and shaped the music to match the words, a major purpose is thwarted when an audience takes no notice of the libretto. Until the singers in the chorus grasp that purpose and follow the thought from words to music, audiences cannot be faulted for their deafness to the text. The obligation of the conductor has been described by Carlo Maria Giulini:

> So we have to deal with mysteries all the time. Our problem is not just how to study the score and learn the notes, but how to read behind the notes and between the lines, and *understand* what a genius wanted to say. We conductors are small men. . . . We are servants, but servants who serve with love, not because we have to, and we must join with these giants' minds and try to feel what they wanted to say.[5]

Singers have similar obligations. If the basic libretto is a biblical text, they need to come alive to its various levels of meanings. The more a chorus becomes a part of the community originally addressed by the text, the better the understanding and the more authentic the musical response. The libretto need not be confined to the Bible; three of the composers I have studied used nonbiblical materials to set up an interchange between a Catholic hymn or a Protestant chorale and the biblical story, a dialogue in which each voice is influenced by its conversational partner.

In requiems and Passion music, the minds of directors, soloists, and chorus should be eager to ponder the ways in which the music expresses Christian thinking about death, and most particularly, the death of Jesus. The music itself calls for increased flexibility in reflection and response. It calls for singers to be open to the composer's message in more than an aesthetic way. This does not mean to eliminate deeper emotions but to stimulate them. I have noted some of the many perceptions of death that the Passion story released among prophets and apostles, perceptions that helped to shape the baseline of Christian thinking. If singers listen to the overtones of the librettos they will detect some of these perceptions and will be better able to articulate them in their singing. For example, when Sir Henry Wood decided to give a performance of a Passion, what he studied first was the story in the Gospel.[6]

In all four works, singers must observe a double movement: from the biblical text to the music, and from the music back to the biblical text. Singers who follow this second movement will discern nuances in the thinking about death that would otherwise escape them. And they will discover many things that their audience will not "hear" in the music. What Theodor Billroth said of the *German Requiem* applies equally to the other works I have discussed:

> One really does not get the proper idea of your creations until he actually takes part in them. When one simply listens, he may find them too massive, too tremendous, too full; one has to take part in them really to assimilate them. *

One final point: the more we restrict the term *death* to its lowest and most neutral common denominator, its meaning in medical terms, the less will we be moved to think or sing about it. Only when we begin to think with Shakespeare about the many deaths created by fear or with the Bible about the many kinds of dying or about our daily little deaths, will we be inclined to turn "passion into sound" and "sound into passion." The more profound the passion, the more convincing the sound. Choruses that sing any of these four works after they have absorbed fully the meanings of the biblical texts may well become deeply aware of the truth that

> Death is the mother of beauty; hence from her,
> Alone, shall come fulfillment to our dreams
> And our desires.[7]

Notes

Prelude

1. George Eliot, "O may I join the choir invisible," in D. J. Enright, ed. and comp., *The Oxford Book of Death* (Oxford: Oxford University Press, 1983), 165.
2. Jacques Barzun, ed., *Pleasures of Music: A Reader's Choice of Great Writing about Music and Musicians from Cellini to Bernard Shaw* (New York: Viking, 1951), 1–2.
3. Elder Olson, "A Recital by Rudolf Serkin," *The American Scholar* [51] (Spring 1982):218.
4. Richard Roberts, *That Strange Man Upon His Cross* (New York: Abingdon, 1934), 122.
5. Albert Schweitzer, *J. S. Bach*, trans. Ernest Newman, 2 vols. (Boston: Bruce Humphries, 1962).
6. Musicians who wish to study the purely musical ways in which composers express the thought of death might well begin with William Kimmel, "The Phrygian Inflection and the Appearances of Death in Music," *College Music Symposium* 20 (Fall 1980):42–76.
7. The following records are recommended: Bach, *St. Matthew Passion* (German), Harmonia Mundi, 1155/7; Brahms, *Requiem* (German) Telarc, 10092-2 and Philips, 6769055; (English) Columbia Records, M25 686; Penderecki, *St. Luke Passion*, EMI 157–99 660/61; Bernstein, *Mass*, Columbia Records, M2 31008.

The Baseline of Christian Thought

1. Elisabeth Kübler-Ross, *On Death and Dying* (New York: Macmillan, 1975), 21.
2. D. J. Enright, ed. and comp., *The Oxford Book of Death* (Oxford: Oxford University Press, 1983).
3. Julius Caesar, act. 2, sc. 2, lines 32–33.
4. Edward Young, "Night Thoughts on Life, Death, and Immortality," in Enright, *Oxford Book of Death*, 29.
5. Paul S. Minear, *New Testament Apocalyptic* (Nashville: Abingdon, 1981), 126–34.

6. Ernest Becker, *The Denial of Death* (New York: Free Press, 1973), 11. See also Paul S. Minear, "The Death of Death: The Carl Michalson Lecture," *The Drew Gateway* 54 (Fall 1983):17–25.

7. Becker, *Denial of Death*, 15.

8. Ibid., 29–30. For a fascinating list of the "names" and "marks" of death, see Walker Percy, *The Second Coming* (New York: Farrar, Straus, Giroux, 1980), 271–74.

9. Paul S. Minear, "Some Pauline Thoughts on Dying: A Study of 2 Corinthians," in *From Faith to Faith: Essays in Honor of Donald G. Miller on His Seventieth Birthday*, ed. Dikran Y. Hadidian (Pittsburgh: Pickwick, 1979), 91–106.

10. Jürgen Moltmann, *The Crucified God: The Cross of Christ as the Foundation and Criticism of Christian Theology*, trans. R. A. Wilson and John Bowden (New York: Harper & Row, 1974), 32–81.

11. Robert C. Tannehill, *Dying and Rising with Christ: A Study in Pauline Theology* (Berlin: Verlag Alfred Töpelmann, 1967).

12. Paul S. Minear, "The Crucified World: the Enigma of Galatians 6.14," in *Theologia Crucis—Signum Crucis: Festschrift für Erich Dinkler zum 70. Geburtstag*, ed. Carl Andresen and Günter Klein (Tübingen: J.C.B. Mohr [Paul Siebeck], 1979), 395–407.

13. Paul S. Minear, "My Peace I Give to You: Toward an Understanding of This Gift," in *Reformed Faith and Politics*, ed. Ronald H. Stone (Washington, D.C.: University Press of America, 1983), 31–48. See also Minear, *John: The Martyr's Gospel* (New York: Pilgrim Press, 1984), 60–62.

14. Laurens van der Post, *A Story Like the Wind* (New York: William Morrow, 1972), 130. The Matabele (or Ndebele), a Bantu-speaking people, live in western Zimbabwe (*The New Columbia Encyclopedia*, s.v. "Matabele").

15. Minear, *New Testament Apocalyptic*, 115–25.

16. Comprehensive analyses of the work of early Christian prophets may be found in M. Eugene Boring, *Sayings of the Risen Jesus: Christian Prophecy in the Synoptic Tradition* (Cambridge: Cambridge University Press, 1982), 58–136.

17. For correlations between prophecy and worship, see D. E. Aune, *The Cultic Setting of Realized Eschatology in Early Christianity* (Leiden: Brill, 1972), 69ff., 101.

18. The Old Testament makes it clear that prophecy had long been associated with music and poetry. In fact, what is probably the oldest recorded song in the Bible is attributed to the prophetess Deborah (Judg. 5). Israel celebrated its liberation from Egypt by cherishing several songs attributed to Moses, the prophet (Exod. 15; Deut. 32; Rev. 15:3). In keeping with Hebrew tradition, in which David and Solomon are considered prophets, I should include many of the psalms as well as the thousand songs attributed to Solomon (1 Kings 4:32). No one challenges the role of Isaiah and Ezekiel as prophets, and both were producers of songs (Isa. 5:1–30; 26:1–21; 42:10–13; Ezek. 33:30–33).

Bach

1. For the structure of the Good Friday service, see Charles Sanford Terry, *Bach: The Passions*, vol. 2, *1729–1731* (London: Oxford University Press, Humphrey Milford, 1926), 6.

2. Paul S. Minear, "Matthew, Evangelist, and Johann, Composer," *Theology Today*, October 1973, 243–55.
3. Otto L. Bettmann, "Bach at Potsdam," *The American Scholar* [52] (Winter 1982–83):83.
4. Paul S. Minear, *Matthew: The Teacher's Gospel* (New York: Pilgrim Press, 1982), 3–7.
5. William H. Scheide, *Johann Sebastian Bach as a Biblical Interpreter* (Princeton: Princeton Theological Seminary, 1952), 10.
6. Ibid., 25.
7. J. Dyer, Program Notes, Handel & Haydn Society, Boston, 1971–72, 22. See also Albert Schweitzer, *J. S. Bach*, trans. Ernest Newman, 2 vols. (Boston: Bruce Humphries, 1962), 2:214–15; and Scheide, *Bach as a Biblical Interpreter*, 26.
8. In this respect Bach shared a common misinterpretation of Matthew. In that Gospel the disciples represented the leaders rather than members of the churches. See Paul S. Minear, "The Disciples and the Crowds in the Gospel of Matthew," *Anglican Theological Review*, Supplementary Series, no. 3 (March 1974):28–44.
9. Martin Dibelius, *Botschaft und Geschichte*, vol. 1, *Zur Evangelienforschung* (Tübingen: J.C.B. Mohr [Paul Siebeck], 1953), 379–80.
10. Paul Steinitz, *Bach's Passions* (New York: Scribner's, 1978), 24, 30.
11. In the manuscript of this as in other works, Bach inscribed the words *Soli Deo Gloria*.
12. The music gives vivid expression of this act of falling; see Steinitz, *Bach's Passions*, 76–77. The intended linkage between this fall and the fall of Adam is established by Helene Werthemann, *Die Bedeutung der alttestamentlichen Historien im Johann Sebastian Bachs Kantaten* (Tübingen: J.C.B. Mohr [Paul Siebeck], 1960), 37.
13. Schweitzer, *J. S. Bach*, 2:36.
14. Steinitz, *Bach's Passions*, 12, 16–17.
15. Will Durant, quoted in Bettmann, "Bach at Potsdam," 82.
16. Steinitz, *Bach's Passions*, 70.
17. Ibid.
18. The translation is by Thomas Dunn, for the Boston Handel & Haydn Society, 1972.
19. Steinitz, *Bach's Passions*, 71; Werthemann, *Die Bedeutung der alttestamentlichen Historien im Johann Sebastian Bachs Kantaten*, 16.
20. Schweitzer, *J. S. Bach*, 2:35.
21. Translation by Dunn, Boston Handel & Haydn Society, 1972.
22. Schweitzer, *J. S. Bach*, 2:211.
23. Percy M. Young, *The Bachs, 1500–1850* (New York: Thomas Y. Crowell, 1970), 101.
24. Paul S. Minear, "Bach and Today's Theologians," *Theology Today*, July 1985, 201–10.

Brahms

1. Albert Schweitzer, *J. S. Bach*, trans. Ernest Newman, 2 vols. (Boston: Bruce Humphries, 1962), 1:254.
2. Richard Specht, *Johannes Brahms*, trans. Eric Blom (New York: E. P. Dut-

ton, 1930), 16; Walter Niemann, *Brahms*, trans. Catherine Alison Phillips (New York: Alfred A. Knopf, 1929), 9.

3. Karl Geiringer, *Brahms: His Life and Work*, 2d ed., rev. and enl. (New York: Oxford University Press, 1947), 328–29. This Bible had been given to Brahms in the year of his birth. "He read it constantly; to the end of his life it remained his book of books . . ." (*The New Grove Dictionary of Music and Musicians*, s.v. "Brahms, Johannes"). See also Brahms' letter to Theodor Billroth, in *Johannes Brahms and Theodor Billroth: Letters from a Musical Friendship*, ed. and trans. Hans Barkan (Norman: University of Oklahoma Press, 1957), 70.

4. M. Kalbeck, *Johannes Brahms* (Berlin, 1904–1914), vol. 2.

5. Paul S. Minear, "Brahms' German Requiem," *Theology Today*, July 1965, 236–49.

6. R. Gerber, "Das Deutsches Requiem als Dokument Brahmscher Frommigkeit," *Das Musikleben* 2 (1979):237–39; see also Geiringer, *Brahms: His Life and Work*, 312–14.

7. Florence May, *The Life of Johannes Brahms*, 2 vols. (London: Edward Arnold, 1905), 393.

8. Ibid.

9. A summary of the vocation and literary style of early Christian prophecy may be found in M. Eugene Boring, *Sayings of the Risen Jesus: Christian Prophecy in the Synoptic Tradition* (Cambridge: Cambridge University Press, 1982), 126–35.

10. Minear, "Brahms' German Requiem," 244–45.

11. This movement was especially valued by Brahms' close friend Theodor Billroth, who expressed a desire that an arrangement of it be used at his funeral (*Brahms and Billroth: Letters from a Musical Friendship*, 94).

12. From the *Notebooks* of Samuel Butler, as quoted in D. J. Enright, ed. and comp., *The Oxford Book of Death* (Oxford: Oxford University Press, 1983), 40. Butler was, of course, misreading both the psalm and the *Requiem* in assuming that both writers were calling for advance notice of the precise date of one's demise. A similar mistake lies at the base of many of Shaw's attacks on the *Requiem*, e.g., "his Requiem is patiently borne only by the corpse" ([George] Bernard Shaw, *Shaw's Music: The Complete Musical Criticism in Three Volumes*, ed. Dan H. Laurence [New York: Dodd, Mead, 1981], 2:93). For additional remarks by Shaw on Brahms' *Requiem*, see ibid., 496, 730.

13. Archibald MacLeish, *Letters of Archibald MacLeish, 1907 to 1982*, ed. R. H. Winnick (Boston: Houghton Mifflin, 1983), 421.

14. *The New Grove Dictionary of Music and Musicians*, s.v. "Brahms, Johannes."

15. Leon R. Kass, "The Case for Mortality," *The American Scholar* [52] (Spring 1983):185–86. It may help us to understand this fusion of finiteness and transcendence in Brahms' own life if we ponder his letter to Theodor Billroth: "It always seems to me a bit melancholy when you write of the feeling of being lonely. I have a thorough understanding for that. . . . For I am that, too. For a long time, or for all time, I have been a bit of a lonely individual and still am!" (*Brahms and Billroth: Letters from a Musical Friendship*, 165).

16. Kalbeck, *Johannes Brahms*.

17. Program Notes to the Requiem, Kennedy Center, Washington, D.C., May 1983, p. 37A—the Program Notes were written by Wayne D. Shirley and excerpts are reprinted with his permission; see also Geiringer, *Brahms: His Life and Work*, 92–93, 101.
18. Paul S. Minear, *New Testament Apocalyptic* (Nashville: Abingdon, 1981), 144–57.
19. Boring, *Sayings of the Risen Jesus*, 126–36.
20. Program Notes to the Requiem, Kennedy Center, Washington, D.C., May 1983, 37A.
21. Ibid.
22. Paul S. Minear, *I Saw a New Earth: An Introduction to the Visions of the Apocalypse* (Washington, D.C.: Corpus Books, 1968), 63–69.
23. Program Notes to the Requiem, Kennedy Center, Washington, D.C., May 1983, 37A.
24. It was entirely appropriate that at the funeral service for Brahms, the Protestant pastor should have used as a benediction the beatitude from movement 7 of the *Requiem* (*Brahms and Billroth: Letters from a Musical Friendship*, 252).
25. May, *Life of Johannes Brahms*, 393.
26. Gerber, "Das Deutsches Requiem," 183.
27. Ibid., 237–39.
28. H. C. Schonberg expressed a judgment very different from that of Gerber: "Very few composers have had equal integrity. Brahms never—never—composed a single note that he did not believe to be a moral and esthetic commitment" ("Low-Key Celebration for a Master," *New York Times Magazine*, 24 April 1983, 90).

Penderecki

1. For a short biographical sketch, see R. Robinson, *Penderecki: A Guide to His Works* (Princeton, N.J.: Prestige, 1983), 1–5.
2. Penderecki, in an interview with R. Robinson, *Ovation*, November 1983, 21.
3. Sorab Modi, *Stagebill*, Kennedy Center, Washington, D.C., November · 1983, 12.
4. Richard Freed, ibid., 19b.
5. Hubert Saal, "The Sound of Poland," *Newsweek*, 17 March 1969, 117.
6. W. Schwinger, *Penderecki* (Stuttgart: Deutsches Verlag, 1979), 206, 214; Herbert Kupferberg, "Passion from Poland," *Atlantic Magazine*, February 1968, 130–32.
7. "Composers: What's the Score?" *Time*, 14 October 1966, 55.
8. Robinson, *Penderecki*, 16.
9. Heinrich Stirnimann, conversation with author, November 1983.
10. For some of the original nuances in John's account, see Paul S. Minear, *John: The Martyr's Gospel* (New York: Pilgrim Press, 1984), 143–52.
11. There may, of course, be other factors, for example, the existence of Penderecki's *Stabat Mater*, which was first performed in Cracow on 27 November 1962 (Schwinger, *Penderecki*, 198–99). The concert at Kennedy Center,

Washington, D.C., in November 1983, showed that this unit can be readily detached from the *Passion*.

12. As an example of Luke's concern with the apostles, see Paul S. Minear, *To Heal and to Reveal: The Prophetic Vocation According to Luke* (New York: Seabury Press, A Crossroads Book, 1976), 122–30.

13. In the New Testament there are four major citations of this psalm (Matt. 27:46; Mark 15:34; John 19:24; Heb. 2:12) and at least a dozen allusions to it.

14. Schwinger, *Penderecki*, 214–15.

15. Modi, *Stagebill*, 11.

16. Attributed to Harry Zelcer, in *Pleasures of Music: A Reader's Choice of Great Writing about Music and Musicians from Cellini to Bernard Shaw*, ed. Jacques Barzun (New York: Viking, 1951), 590.

17. *The New Grove Dictionary of Music and Musicians*, s.v. "Penderecki, Krzysztof."

18. Schwinger, *Penderecki*, 204–5.

19. Roland de Pury, *Journal from My Cell*, trans. Barrows Mussey (New York: Harper & Bros., 1946), 21.

20. Schwinger, *Penderecki*, 213.

21. David J. Graybill, in a letter to the author.

Bernstein

1. Leonard Bernstein, *The Joy of Music* (New York: Simon & Schuster, 1959), 226, 242.

2. "Could the eclectic age—borrowing everywhere from the Bible to *Porgy and Bess*, from Beethoven to the world of *Hair*, from the symbolic body and blood of Christ to sheerest humanism—shape an enduring musical tribute to human failure and aspiration, to divine inspiration and its loss? . . . nothing less than that was Leonard Bernstein's high intention" (William Bender, "A Mass for Everyone, Maybe," *Time*, 20 September 1971, 41).

3. According to the original program notes, *Mass* "came to exist because the composer believes that the crisis of faith is the principal crisis of our century" (quoted in C. J. McNaspy, "Bernstein's 'Mass' Opens Kennedy Center, I: Against Odds, It Came Off Well," *America*, 25 September 1971, 228. Such an intention surely establishes kinship between Bernstein and biblical authors.

4. The archbishop of Cincinnati was quoted in "The Talk of the Town" as saying that Bernstein's *Mass* is "a blatant sacrilege against all we hold sacred" (*New Yorker*, 10 June 1972, 25).

5. Paul S. Minear, "Leonard Bernstein: Theologian," *Andover Newton Quarterly* 17 (March 1977):281–89.

6. John Gallen, "Bernstein's 'Mass' Opens Kennedy Center, II: The 'Mass'— Successful Liturgy?" *America*, 25 September 1971, 229.

7. This is characteristic of all four of the composers I studied. In setting a biblical text to music, they assumed its full contemporaneity. Most professional biblical exegetes today begin with the opposite assumption.

8. Compare Penderecki's treatment of the same phrase in ch. 4.

9. Here may lie a basic difference between secular America and Catholic Poland. Penderecki can assume that his audience will recognize the bond be-

tween Jesus and all other men, forged by his death; Bernstein's audience finds such recognition impossible.

10. John Ardoin makes an astute comment. Observing that there are two Bernsteins, the secular Bernstein of the New York music (e.g., *On the Waterfront*) and the sacred Bernstein of the *Chicester Psalms*, he writes that the two "have come together as equals in only one piece so far—Mass . . ." ("Leonard Bernstein at Sixty: The Many Careers, the Singular Man," *High Fidelity*, August 1978, 57).

11. Cheryl A. Forbes, "Bernstein's 'Mass': No Word From the Lord," *Christianity Today*, 8 October 1971, 40.

12. The genius of *Mass* stems in part from the honest and uncompromising juxtaposition of the denial of peace and its gift. In this respect *Mass* is comparable to the *War Requiem* of Benjamin Britten. To articulate the never-ending denial of peace, Bernstein relies on the anguished cries of many individuals and the climactic mob scenes on the stage. Britten accomplishes a similar effect by relying on the poems of a single casualty of World War I, Wilfred Owen, who served as spokesman for "these who die like cattle." In both works the denial of peace makes the prayers for peace all the more powerful and the gift of peace, however problematic, all the more redemptive.

13. Hubert Saal attributes to Bernstein words that may indicate his conception of *Mass*. God is "the thing people can't live without from day to day. That's what faith is, the God in you. When people lose touch with that, despair sets in and the result is withdrawal from life, by suicide or drugs or just by becoming passive and uninvolved. That's what the song 'Easy' is all about and what the last scene is all about. Everybody has to look within himself to find God, not in the organized trappings of religion. Then you can relate to someone else, then to a group, then to society" ("A Celebration of the Spirit," *Newsweek*, 20 September 1971, 30 [Copyright 1971, by Newsweek, Inc. All Rights Reserved. Reprinted by Permission]).

Postlude

1. Amos Niven Wilder, *Theopoetic: Theology and the Religious Imagination* (Philadelphia: Fortress Press, 1976), 1.

2. Walt Whitman, *Leaves of Grass*, ed. Emory Holloway (Garden City, N.Y.: Doubleday, Doran, 1943), 183.

3. Albert Schweitzer, *J. S. Bach*, trans. Ernest Newman, 2 vols. (Boston: Bruce Humphries, 1962), 1:viii. Paul Jordan, stressing the same point, has remarked that some of Bach's choral works "remain relatively impenetrable, musically speaking, until their verbal or pictorial symbolism has been illuminated" ("Helmut Walcha: Artist-Teacher," *College Music Symposium* 22 [Fall 1982]:153). For this note I am indebted to Jan Forman.

4. P. E. Vernon, "The Ear Is Not Enough," in *Pleasures of Music: A Reader's Choice of Great Writing about Music and Musicians from Cellini to Bernard Shaw*, ed. Jacques Barzun (New York: Viking, 1951), 186–87.

5. "Carlo Maria Giulini," in *Maestro: Encounters with Conductors of Today*, ed. Helena Matheopoulos (New York: Harper & Row, 1982), 170.

6. Paul Steinitz, *Bach's Passions* (New York: Scribner's, 1978), 117–18.

7. Wallace Stevens, "Sunday Morning," in *The Collected Poems of Wallace Stevens* (New York: Alfred A. Knopf, 1968), 68–69.